# PRAYER WARFARE AGAINST 70 MAD SPIRITS

DR. D. K. OLUKOYA

PRAYER WARFARE AGAINST SEVENTY MAD SPIRITS



ISBN 978-36917-0-8
Reprinted May, 2017
Reprinted October, 2019

Published by:

**The Battle Cry Christian Ministries**

322, Herbert Macaulay Way, Sabo, Yaba
P.O.Box 12272, Ikeja, Lagos.
Website: www.battlecrystores.com
email: info@batlecrystores.com
customercare@battlecrystores.com
sales@battlecrystores.com
Phone: 0803-304-4239, 0816-122-9775

I salute my wonderful wife, Pastor Shade, for her invaluable support in the ministry.

I appreciate her unquantifiable support in the book ministry as the cover designer, art editor and art adviser.



Printed in Nigeria.
Scripture quotations are taken from the Holy Bible, King James Version
Cover illustration: Sister Shade Olukoya

# Contents

## Table of Contents

## DEDICATION

This Prayer Book is dedicated to Late Apostle Joseph Ayodele Babalola, a minister of God who understood the power of prayer. He was the man mightily used by God to ignite the fire of the first Christian revival in this country in the nineteen thirties.

Apostle J. A. Babalola easily stands out as the pioneer of the Pentecostal movement in Nigeria and the African continent. The mighty revival he spearheaded in the 1930s has become a watershed and reference point in the annals of Christianity in Nigeria and beyond. His evangelical drive was aggressive, his commitment to holiness exemplary and his demonstration of the power of God over evil forces overwhelming. This ignited a revival fire that spread around the West African sub-region.

Brother J. A. and his team of aggressive evangelists and prayer warriors entered forbidden forests, silenced demons that demanded worship, paralysed deeply-rooted anti-gospel activities, emptied hospitals by the healing power of the Lord Jesus Christ, rendered witchdoctors jobless and started the first indigenous Holy-Ghost filled church in Nigeria. So far - and we stand to be corrected- none has equalled, let alone surpassed this humble Brother in the field of aggressive evangelism in this country.

Babalola's revival came at a time when the African continent was deep into idolatry or at best, Christian orthodoxy. God used him to bring the reality of salvation, healing, deliverance and unspeakable joy to a population hitherto overwhelmed by darkness. . His ministry ushered in a fundamental change in religion as understood by the people.

Apostle Joseph Ayodele Babalola indeed changed the face Christianity in Nigeria and planted what has today made Nigeria one of the world's most evangelised countries.

# INTRODUCTION

Prayer is a gift from God to you and a privilege. The gift is offered to all and all may become the wielders of the great power in prayer However, the fact remains that the power of prayer is least exercised by the average believer. You will do well to learn the art of warfare prayer. The present prayer temperature of many Christians needs to rise if they expect serious breakthroughs.

The prayer points in this book are targeted at certain needs so that as you are praying you will not be beating the air. This is how to use the book:

Locate your area of need by looking at the table of contents. Select the appropriate Scriptures promising you what you desire. Meditate on them and let them sink into your spirit.

Go about the prayers in any of the following ways as led by the Holy Spirit:

Three consecutive days' vigil, i.e praying from 10 P.M. to 5 A.M.

Three days' fast (breaking daily), i.e. praying at intervals and breaking the fast at 6.00 P.M. or 9.00.P.M. daily.

Seven days' vigil, i.e. praying from 10 P.M. to 5 A.M. seven consecutive nights.

Seven days' fast (breaking daily), i.e. praying at intervals and breaking the fast at 6.00 P. M. or 9.00.P.M. daily

Three or more days of dry fast i.e praying and fasting three or more days without any food or drink.
Pray aggressively.

***NOTE:*** Spend part of the vigil or fasting praying in the Spirit:

Praying in the Spirit is an ability to pray in tongues as given utterance by the Holy Spirit. To pray in the Spirit, you must have been baptised in the Holy Ghost (not water baptism) - 1 Cor. 14:15.

You will be victorious in Jesus' name. Amen!

# VIOLENCE AGAINST 70 MAD SPIRITS

Rev. 12:12: Therefore rejoice, *ye* heavens, and ye that dwell in them Woe to the inhabiters of the earth and of the sea! for the devil is come down unto you, having great wrath, because he knoweth that he hath but a short time.

Rev, 16:13-14: And I saw three unclean spirits like frogs *come* out
of the mouth of the dragon, and out of the mouth of the beast, and
out of the mouth of the false prophet. 14 For they are the spirits of
devils, working miracles, *which* go forth unto the kings of the earth
and of the whole world, to gather them to the battle of that great day
of God Almighty.

Matthew 11:12: And from the days of John the Baptist until now the kingdom of heaven suffereth violence, and the violent take it by force.

2 Tim 3:13: But evil men and seducers shall wax worse and worse, deceiving, and being deceived.

Psalm 2:1-12: Why do the heathen rage, and the people imagine a
vain thing? 2 The kings of the earth set themselves, and the rulers take
counsel together, against the LORD, and against his anointed, *saying*
4 He that sitteth in the heavens shall laugh: the Lord shall have them
in derision. 5 Then shall he speak unto them in his wrath, and vex them
in his sore displeasure. 6 Yet have I set my king upon my holy hill of
Zion. 7 I will declare the decree: the LORD hath said unto me, Thou *art*
my Son; this day have I begotten thee, 8 Ask of me, and I shall give
thee the heathen for thine inheritance, and the uttermost parts of
the earth *for* thy possession. 9 Thou shalt break them with a rod of
iron: thou shalt dash them in pieces like a potter's vessel. 10 Be wise
now therefore, O ye kings: be instructed, ye judges of the earth.
11 Serve the LORD with fear, and rejoice with trembling. 12 Kiss the Son,
lest he be angry, and ye perish *from* the way, when his wrath is kindled
but a little Blessed *are* all they that put their trust in him.

Psalm 7::6: Arise, O LORD, in thine anger, lift up thyself because of the rage of mine enemies: and awake for me to the judgment *that* thou hast commanded.

There is a raging battle going on. This battle is between right and the wrong: between light and darkness, real and counterfeit, evil and good, negative and positive. It is a battle of which no one can be neutral. We are born into it and we've got no choice. You cannot opt out. There is nowhere to go. The world is not like a bus which you can stop and get off. You are in it, you are part of it.

Satan is an obstinate fighter, who yields only when he must.

The enemy has poured a legion of angry spirits into the world. These spirits act in a rage, and exhibit unthinkable madness and wickedness.

In spite of their rage, they do their evil with superb intelligence and purpose. They operate with malice and hatred, determination, undeviating persistence and skill.

They get very angry when they see a believer who understands the art of spiritual warfare.

Spiritual violence is needed. You must have violent anxiety. You must burst forth with holy anger, violent determination and faith.

You must also possess holy fury, fierceness, rage and madness. No soul that ever cried violently to God has been disappointed.

Violent prayers that are raised to the throne of God, always have the answers.

**You must not hold your peace.**

# WHAT ARE MAD SPIRITS?

They are:

1. Spirits that are resistant to command
2. Spirits that operate with terrible anger
3. Spirits that threaten and boast
4. Spirits that speak strange voices to victim's ears
5. Spirits that attack in the dreams
6. Spirits sponsored by satanic agents
7. Spirits sponsored by incantations
8. Spirits sponsored by curses and covenants
9. Spiritual armed robbers
10. Spirits that disrespect geographical locations
11. Spirits whose mission is to kill and to destroy
12. Envying spirits
13. Spirits that roam around the garden of life, looking for ways to penetrate
14. Barking spirits
15. Battle ready spirits
16. Spirits that wage hot battle at the edge of breakthroughs
17. Swallowing spirits
18. Organised attackers
19. Spirits on assignment to hinder at all cost
20. Police dog spirits sniffing out preys
21. Stubborn, pursuing spirits

# WEAPONS OF SPIRITUAL WARFARE

These are:

1. Whirlwind
2. Fire of God
3. Great earthquake
4. Sea-quake
5. Air-quake
6. Horrible tempest
7. Furnace of affliction
8. Thunder and fire
9. Brimstone and fire
10. Destructive oppression
11. Unbearable heat
12. Concentrated acid
13. Destroying flood
14. Great furnace
15. Shock
16. Destruction
17. Anger of the Lord
18. Bread of affliction
19. Water of affliction
20. Red-hot charcoal
21. Cloud of sorrow

22. Raging fire
23, Blindness
24. Madness
25. Worms
26. Continuous plagues
27. Fear of day and night
28. Bitter destruction
29. Double destruction
30. Self-destruction
31 Disappointment
32. Failures
33. Discomfort on all sides
34. Disorderliness
35. Hail and fire mingled with the blood of the Lamb
36. Confusion
37. Blood of Jesus
38. Testimony
39. Preaching
40. Word of God
41. Angels of the Lord
42. Praises

# MAD SPIRITS

1. Problem expanders
2. Star hijackers
3. Progress arresters
4. Poverty activators
5, Coffin spirits
6. Vagabond spirits
7. Evil observers
8. Satanic arrows
9. Desert spirits
10, Evil markers
11. Business bewitchers
12. Marriage killers
13. Spiritual marriages
14. Arrows of infirmity
15. Shame distributors
16. Territorial demoters
17. Occult arrows
18. Satanic poison
19. Dream manipulators
20. Satanic programmers
21. Wicked terminators
22. Backsliding spirits
23. Seductive spirits
24. Rock demons
25. Forest demons
26. Spirit of death and hell
27. Affliction revivers
28. Spirits of divination
29. Devouring spirit
30. Spiritual gunmen
31. Breakthrough amputators
32. Tragedy activators
33. Curse enforcing spirits
34. Children killers
35. Womb polluters
36. Helper manipulators
37. Ministry destroyers
38. Spirit of Jezebel
39. Spirit of slumber
40. Spirit of infirmity
41. Spirit of jealousy
42. Familiar spirit
43. Witchcraft
44. Wicked spirits

45. Spirit of error
46. Anti-Christ spirit
47. Spirit of oppression
48. Spirit of bondage
49. Sorrowful spirit
50. Spirit of fear
51. Spirit of insanity
52. Spirit of heaviness
53. Spirit of injury
54. Spirit of whoredom
55. Haughty spirit
56. Lying spirit
57. Unclean spirit
58. Deaf and dumb spirit
59. Spirit of the world
60. Spirit of treachery
61. Spirit of murder
62. Perverse Spirit
63. Eaters of flesh and drinkers of blood
64. Compulsive eating spirits
65. Spirits of failure
66. Suicide spirits
67. Stress spirit
68. Rebellion spirit
69. Destructive addictions spirit
70. Spirit of Polygamy

# 1

# PROBLEM EXPANDERS

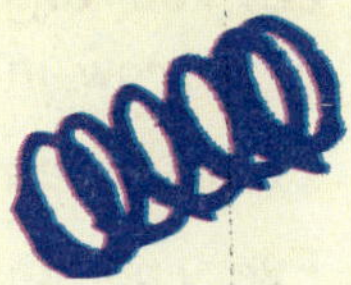

## INTRODUCTION

Problem expanders are powers that multiply sorrows. They are powers that take an inch of trouble and convert them to a mile. They expand unprofitable situations. For example, they made Saul tear Samuel's garment.

## PRAISE WORSHIP

## PRAYER WARFARE

1. Every power prolonging affliction in my life, I bury you today, in the name of Jesus.
2. Every problem expander, I kill your power today, in Jesus' name.
3. I shall go from glory to glory and from strength to strength, in the name of Jesus
4. The enemy will not measure my length on the ground, in the name of Jesus
5. Holy Ghost, arise and deliver me from every evil cage, in the name of Jesus
6. I decree an end to every witchcraft affliction, in Jesus' name.
7. I must experience total deliverance by the power in the blood of Jesus.
8. Every lion of death crouching to attack me, die, in Jesus' name.
9. Thou power of backwardness, lose your power, in Jesus' name.

10. By the thunder of Your power, O Lord, kill the power behind my problems, in the name of Jesus.
11. Let the finger of God arise and disgrace every power working against my peace, in the name of Jesus.
12. Let Your angels arise, O Lord, and cut off every umbilical cord of sorrow, in the name of Jesus.
13. I dismantle every chain-problem, in the name of Jesus.
14. Every power magnetizing any problem to me, loose your hold, in the name of Jesus.
15. I must arise and shine, in the name of Jesus.
16. Every evil tarrying at the bus stop of darkness, die, in the name of Jesus.
17. I shall not die in problems, my problems shall surrender, in the name of Jesus.
18. O yoke from the heaven lies and the sea, break by fire, in the name of Jesus.
19. O God arise with Your arm of strength and deliver me speedily. in the name of Jesus.
20. Power of the oppressor, perish by fire, in Jesus' name.
21. Let my glory arise and refuse to listen to the voice of any problem, in the name of Jesus.
22. Fire of God, burn to ashes every altar of affliction raised against me, in the name of Jesus.
23. Power to cross my Jordan, fall on me now, in Jesus name.

# 2

# STAR HIJACKERS

## INTRODUCTION

Every one has a star which can be caged, suppressed or hijacked by spiritual star hunters. The wise men saw the star of the Lord Jesus Christ in the East and followed it. When you have a colourful destiny, the enemy may monitor your progress and attempt to cast down and demobilize your star. Evil wise men may also be hired against you after the order of Balaam to curse and pull you down.

## PRAISE WORSHIP

## PRAYER WARFARE

1. Holy Ghost fire, anise and damage every resistance to the glow of my star, in the name of Jesus,
2. Thou star demoters, receive the sword of fire, in Jesus' name.
3. I recover my star from the cage of star hunters, in Jesus' name.
4. I rise above every dark sentence issued against my star, in the name of Jesus.
5. Let the pattern of darkness be broken to pieces, in Jesus' name.
6. I put to flight, every organised warfare against my star, in the name of Jesus.

7. Every pit dug to swallow my star, be covered by the blood of Jesus.
8. Let the star of my destiny pick up fire and overtake its contemporaries, in the name of Jesus.
9. Every evil wise man observing the star of my destiny, receive blindness, in the name of Jesus.
10. Every power of the valley, die, in the name of Jesus.
11. I destroy every spell and jinx placed upon my star, in Jesus' name. Let the power of God move me forward by fire, in Jesus' name.

# 3

## PROGRESS ARRESTERS

### INTRODUCTION

These are powers working after the order of the soldiers sent to arrest Elijah and Elisha. A person progresses for a while, then unforseen circumstances arise, which completely paralyse his progress. The result is continuous history of frustration, confusion and profitless hard-work. Candidates of progress arresters are always blamed for one thing or the other instead of being commended.

## PRAISE WORSHIP

## CONFESSIONS

**Deut 28:13:** And the LORD shall make thee the head, and not the tail: and thee shalt be above only, and thou shalt not be beneath: if that thou hearken unto the commandments of the LORD thy God, which I command thee this day, to observe and to do them.

**Prov 21:4:** The king's heart is in the hand of the LORD, as the rivers of water he turneth it whithersoever he will.

**1 Sam 7:45-46:** Then said David to the Philistine, Thou comest to me with a sword, and with a spear, and with a shield: but I come to thee in the name of the LORD of hosts, the God of the armies of Israel, whom thou hast defied. This day will the LORD deliver thee into mine hand; and I will smite thee, and take thine head from thee: and I will give the carcases of the host of the Philistines this day unto the fowls of the air, and to the wild beasts of the earth; that all the earth may know that there is a God in Israel.

**Deut 33:25-27:** Thy shoes shall be iron and brass; and as thy days, so shall my strength be. There is none like unto the God of Jeshurun. who rideth upon the heaven in thy help, and in his excellency on the sky. The eternal God is thy refuge, and underneath are the everlasting arms: and he shall thrust out the enemy from before thee; and shall say, Destroy them.

**Jer. 1:19:** And they shall fight against thee; but they shall not prevail against thee; for I am with thee, saith the LORD, to deliver thee.

**Nahum 1:7-8:** The LORD is good, a strong hold in the day of trouble: and he knoweth them that trust in him. But with an overrunning flood he will make an utter end of the place thereof, and darkness shall pursue his enemies.

**Ps 75:6:** For promotion cometh neither from the east, nor from the west nor from the south.

**Ps 113:5,7-8:** Who is like unto the LORD our God, who dwelleth on high. He raiseth up the poor out of the dust, and lifteth the needy out of the dunghill: That he may set him with princes, even with the princes of his people.

**Phil. 4:13,19:** I can do all things through Christ which strengtheneth me. Bu my God shall supply all your need according to his riches in glory by Christ Jesus.

**Gal. 6:17** From henceforth let no man trouble me: for I bear in my body the marks of the Lord Jesus.

**PRAYER WARFARE**

1. Thank the Lord because He alone is the unstoppable progress.
2. Father, empower me to find favour in the sight of my divine helpers, in the name of Jesus.
3. Let all the demonic obstacles that have been established in the

heart of my divine helpers against my prosperity, be destroyed, in the name of Jesus.

4. I silence and put to flight, all the spirits of fear, anxiety and discouragement, in the name of Jesus.
5. Lord, let divine wisdom fall upon all who are supporting me in these matters.
6. I break the backbone of any spirit of conspiracy and treachery, in the name of Jesus.
7. Lord, hammer my matter into the minds of those who will assist me, so that they do not suffer from demonic loss of memory.
8. I paralyse the handwork of household enemies and envious agents in this matter, in the name of Jesus.
9. Let all evil competitors stumble and fall, in Jesus' name.
10. Let all my adversaries make mistakes that will advance my cause, in the name of Jesus.
11. Let all the adversaries of my breakthroughs be put to shame, the name of Jesus.
12. I claim the power to overcome and to excel above all competitors, in the name of Jesus.
13. Let any decision by any Panel be favourable unto me, in the name of Jesus.
14. Every negative word and pronouncement against my success, be completely nullified, in Jesus' name.
15. All competitors with me in this issue, will find my defeat unattainable, in the name of Jesus.
16. I claim supernatural wisdom, to answer all questions in a way that

will advance my cause, in the name of Jesus.

17. I confess my sin of exhibiting occasional doubts.
18. I bind every spirit manipulating my beneficiaries against me. in the name of Jesus.
19. I remove my name from the book of dreamers of goodness without realisation, in the name of Jesus.
20. Let the cloud blocking the sunlight of my glory and breakthrough be dispersed, in the name of Jesus.
21. Lord, let wonderful changes begin to be my lot from this week.
22. I reject every spirit of the tail in all areas of my life, in the name of Jesus.
23. Oh Lord, bring me into favour with all those who will decide on my advancement.
24. Oh Lord, cause a divine substitution to happen if this is what will move me ahead.
25. I reject the spirit of the tail and I claim the spirit of the head, in the name of Jesus.
26. I command all evil records planted by the devil in anyone's mind against my advancement to be shattered to pieces. in Jesus' name.
27. Oh Lord, transfer, remove or change all human agents who are bent on stopping my advancement.
28. Oh Lord, smoothen my path to the top by your hand of fire.
29. I receive the anointing to excel above my contemporaries, in the name of Jesus.
30. Lord, catapult me to greatness as You did for Daniel in the land of Babylon.

31. Lord, help me to identify and deal with any weakness in me that can hinder my progress.

32. I bind every strongman delegated to hinder my progress, in the name of Jesus.

33. Oh Lord, despatch Your angels to roll away every stumbling block to my promotion, advancement and elevation.

34. Let power change hands in my place of work, to the hands of the Holy Spirit.

35. Let the fire of God consume any rock tying me down to the same spot, in the name of Jesus.

36. All demonic chains preventing my advancement, be broken, in the name of Jesus.

37. All human agents delaying / denying my advancement, I bind the evil spirits controlling your minds, in the name of Jesus.

38. Holy Spirit, direct the decisions of any panel in my favour, in the name of Jesus.

39. I refuse to fail at the edge of my miracle, in Jesus' name.

40. O Lord, release Your angels to fight my battle.

41. Let warrior angels be released to fight my battles in the heavenlies, in the name of Jesus.

42. I bind every deception and manipulation targeted against my life, in the name of Jesus.

43. O Lord, let the rain of... (pick from the following) fall upon my life in abundance.

- love - power
- sound mind
- knowledge
- understanding
- revelation
- wisdom

- freedom
- deliverance
- boldness
- zealousness
- purity
- holiness
- excellence
- praise
- joy
- peace
- longsuffering
- gentleness
- goodness
- faith
- word of wisdom
- word of knowledge
- might
- healing
- working of miracles
- prophecy
- discerning of spirits
- divers kinds of tongues
- interpretation of tongues
- grace
- mercy
- life
- health
- restoration
- well-being
- counsel
- strength

44. Thank You, Lord, for setting in motion the machinery for my advancement.

# 4

# POVERTY ACTIVATORS

## INTRODUCTION

These are powers that activate poverty and wretchedness. They bring bankruptcy into profitable ventures. They introduce 'rat' workers into businesses. When they are at work, any attempt to generate wealth eventually ends up in the history book of failure.

## PRAISE WORSHIP

## PRAYER WARFARE

1 Let every parental mistake affecting my life be reversed, in the name of Jesus.
2. O God, arise and let my head be lifted up, in Jesus' name.
3. Every witchcraft-sponsored poverty, die, in Jesus' name.
4. Every altar of poverty in my place of birth working against my prosperity, burn to ashes, in Jesus' name.
5. Every satanic priest, ministering against my prosperity on any evil altar, die by fire, in the name of Jesus.
6. Every strength and power of environmental altar wishing against my life, wither, in the name of Jesus.
7. Today, I raise the altar of continuous prosperity upon my destiny, in the name of Jesus.

8. Every stronghold of physical and spiritual poverty in my life. be pulled down by fire, in the name of Jesus

9. Any covenant in my life that is strengthening the stronghold of poverty, break, in the name of Jesus.

10. Every stronghold of poverty where I am living now and in my place of work, I pull you down, in Jesus' name.

11. O Lord, create opportunities for my prosperity today.

12. I bind and cast out, every negative word enforcing poverty upon my life, in the name of Jesus.

13. Spirit of stinginess, disappear from my life, in Jesus' name.

14. I bind and cast out, the spirit of disobedience, in Jesus'

15. Where other people are spending money, I refuse to spend boldface, in the name of Jesus.

16. Every evil machinery against my prosperity, be destroyed, in the name of Jesus.

17. I destroy by fire every weapon of poverty targeted against my life, in the name of Jesus.

18. Every descendant of poverty in my life, fall down and die, in the name of Jesus.

19 Every evil power sitting on my prosperity, somersault and die, in the name of Jesus.

20. I break every caldron of poverty in my life, in Jesus' name.

21. You stronghold of poverty, receive the fire of God, in Jesus name.

22. I cut myself and my family off from every inherited poverty, In the name of Jesus.

29. Prayer Warfare Against 70 Mad Spirits

23. Every stigma of poverty in my life, be robbed off by the blood of Jesus.

24. Every adjustment to humiliate me, I rebel against you, in the name of Jesus.

25. Every power adjusting my life to poverty, fall down and die, in the name of Jesus.

26. I shall not adjust to poverty, in the name of Jesus.

27. Holy Spirit, adjust my life to prosperity, in Jesus' name.

28. You network chains of failure rattling my life, melt by fire, in the name of Jesus.

29. You anchor of failure holding my destiny, break, in Jesus' name.

30. Every spiritual chain of slavery upon my life, break by fire, in the name of Jesus.

31. Every chain of inherited failure upon my life, break by fire, in the name of Jesus.

32. Let every evil seed of generational poverty dry up, in Jesus' name

33. I command the stronghold of inherited poverty in my life to be pulled down by the blood of Jesus.

34. Holy Ghost, arrest on my behalf every spirit of poverty, in the name of Jesus.

35. I dismantle every demonic opposition to my prosperity, in the name of Jesus.

36. Every satanic river of poverty and failure, dry up by fire, in the name of Jesus.

37. Every altar of poverty prepared by my ancestors, break now, in the name of Jesus.

38. Every witchcraft assembly in my neighbourhood, be scattered Holy Ghost fire, in the name of Jesus.
39. Let the stubborn strongman of poverty in my place of birth (mention the place) be paralysed by fire, in Jesus' name.
40. Every territorial spirit working against my prosperity, be chained in the name of Jesus.
41. Every covenant made at my birth and in my place of birth, break in the name of Jesus.
42. Every witchcraft covenant of poverty affecting my prosperity. break, in the name of Jesus.
43. Every covenant of poverty made by the living or the dead against my prosperity, break, in the name of Jesus.
44. Hear, O heavens, I am dead to the covenant of poverty, I am alive to the covenant of prosperity, in Jesus' name.
45. Every arrow of poverty fired into my life, come out with all your roots, in the name of Jesus.
46. Every curse of poverty placed upon my family, be consumed by fire, in the name of Jesus.
47. Every curse of poverty fired into my life by household wickedness, go back to your sender, in the name of Jesus.
48. As a result of my prosperity prayers, I receive the mandate to enter into the covenant of wealth, in Jesus' name.
49. O Lord, empower me to pluck the seed of wealth that will swallow poverty in my life.
50. From today, my portion in life has changed from that of a beggar and borrower to that of a lender and giver, in Jesus' name.

51. Every sponsored dream of poverty by household wickedness against my life, vanish, in the name of Jesus.
52. Every satanic banker representing me in the spirit world, fall down and die, in the name of Jesus.
53. Every evil bank established against my destiny, be liquidated by fire, in the name of Jesus.
54. Every Egyptian poverty, I shall see you no more, in Jesus' name.
55. I command the thunder of God to break into pieces, all the satanic arrows of poverty fired into my life, in Jesus' name.
56. Every foundational arrow of poverty, be removed by fire, in the name of Jesus.
57. I paralyse, all the inherited arrows of poverty, in Jesus' name.
58. Father Lord, shield me against any arrow of poverty, in the name of Jesus.
59. Every cage of poverty, roast to ashes, in Jesus' name.
60. Every satanic barrier designed to hold me back from my desired position, be shattered to pieces, in Jesus' name.
61. Every instrument of failure working against my advancement, I command you to fail, in Jesus' name.
62. Let every evil decree working against my potentials be revoked, in the name of Jesus.
63. I remove by fire every mark of poverty in my life, in Jesus' name.
64. My life, my business, reject all marks of poverty, in Jesus' name.
65. Every evil hand that carried me when I was a baby, roast by fire, in the name of Jesus.
66. You mountain of debt, programmed to put me into poverty, be

Cast away, in the name of Jesus

67. I recover my placenta from the cage of wicked people, in the in the name of Jesus.
68. Every agent attached to profitlessness in my life, be paralysed, in the name of Jesus.
69. I receive divine direction, in the name of Jesus.
70. O Lord, give me divine revelation.
71. O Lord, let Your glory overshadow every work that I do.
72. O God arise, and disgrace every trap of poverty in my family, in the name of Jesus.
73. O God arise, and scatter every trap of poverty in my life, in the name of Jesus.
74. The labour of my hands shall prosper, in the name of Jesus.
75. Every waster of my prosperity, be impotent, in Jesus' name.
76. Every known and unknown opposer of my comfort, be paralysed, in the name of Jesus.
77. Anything planted in my life to disgrace me, come out with all your roots, in the name of Jesus.
78. I reject demonic stagnation of my blessings, in Jesus' name.
79. I reject weak financial breakthroughs. I claim big financial breakthroughs, in the name of Jesus.
80. Every hidden and clever devourer, be bound, in Jesus' name.
81. I release myself from every family pattern of poverty, in the name of Jesus.
82 I refuse to allow my wealth to die on any evil altar, in Jesus name.

83. I reject every prosperity paralysis, in the name of Jesus.
84. I possess all my foreign benefits today, in Jesus' name.
85. My pocket will not leak, in the name of Jesus.
86. I dash every poverty dream to the ground, in Jesus' name.
87. Every good thing that my hands have started to build, they shall finish it, in the name of Jesus.
88. I refuse to become the foot-mat of amputators, in Jesus' name.
89. Let my helpers appear, let my hindrances disappear, in the name of Jesus.
90. God of providence, raise divine capital for me, in Jesus' name.
91. I occupy my rightful position, in the name of Jesus.
92. Every delayed and denied prosperity, manifest by fire, in the name off Jesus.
93. Every bewitched account, receive deliverance, in Jesus' name.
94. Every snail anointing on my blessings, fall down and die, in the name of Jesus.
95. Every power broadcasting my goodness for evil, be silenced, in the name of Jesus.
96. I refuse to lock the doors of blessings against myself, in the name of Jesus.
97. I release myself from every spirit of poverty, in Jesus' name.
98. I curse the spirit of poverty with the curse of the Lord, in Jesus' name.
99. I release myself from every bondage of poverty, in Jesus' name.
100. The riches of the gentiles shall come to me, in Jesus' name.

101. Let divine magnets of prosperity be planted in my hands, in the name of Jesus.

102. I retrieve my purse from the hand of Judas, in Jesus' name.

103. Let there be a reverse transfer of my satanically transferred wealth, in the name of Jesus.

104. I take over the wealth of sinners, in Jesus' name.

105. I recover the steering wheel of my wealth from the hands of evil drivers, in the name of Jesus.

106. O Lord, revive my blessings by Your fire.

107. O Lord, return my stolen blessings unto me a million-fold.

108. O Lord, send out the angels of God to bring me blessings.

109. Whatever needs changing in my life to bring me blessings, be changed by fire now, in the name of Jesus.

110. Every power sitting on my wealth, fall down and die, in the name of Jesus.

111. I shall not be moved, but my mountain shall be moved, in the name of Jesus.

112. I shall not give up but my problem shall give up, in Jesus' name.

113. My problem shall surrender, in the name of Jesus.

114. I receive the sprinkling of the blood of Jesus into even department of my life, in the name of Jesus.

115. I set judgment against every evil altar erected against my destiny, in the name of Jesus,

116. O Lord, release my tongue to prosper.

117. O Lord, take Your place as Lord in my family.

118. I receive the power to move my mountains, in Jesus' name.

119. Problems, pack your load and leave my life now, in Jesus' name.

120 Every satanic perfume that covers the glory of God in my life, be wiped off by the blood of Jesus.

121. Every demonic blanket that covers my star, I tear you destroy you, in the name of Jesus.

122. My star, must rise and shine clearly, in the name of Jesus.

123. My king shall reign, in the name of Jesus.

124. Oh Lord, send Your angels to dig out and destroy every evil root in my life.

125. Every wicked weapon fashioned against my life, backfire against the enemy, in the name of Jesus.

126. Today, I demand seven-fold restitution from satan, in the name of Jesus.

## INTRODUCTION

These are terrible ancestral spirits that pursue victims relentlessly with thoughts of death, personal destruction, suicide and a completely negative view of life. When plagued by these spirits, dreams of dead persons, funerals, coffins, cemeteries, will be a common occurrence. The general life will be a life of a living corpse. The victim will not operate in the right position in life but will always operate at the tail region. In many situations these victims are walking time bombs, waiting to explode.

# 5

# COFFIN SPIRITS

**PRAISE WORSHIP**

**PRAYER WARFARE**

1. I refuse to accept a satanic substitute for my destiny, in the name of Jesus.
2. (Lay your right hand on your head. Under normal situation, this is the part of your body that first came out of your mother), I challenge my head with the fire of the Holy Ghost, in Jesus' name.
3. Every strange hand, placed on my head, roast, in Jesus' name.
4. Let my head be released from every curse, in Jesus' name.

5. Every curse placed upon my life by my parents, either seriously or jokingly, blood of Jesus, wipe it away now.
6 Every curse placed upon my life by my wife / husband, blood of Jesus, wipe it away now.
7. Any curse issued upon my life by my former evil friends, be wiped away by the blood of Jesus.
8. If my head has been manipulated away from my place of blessings, let it be released now, in the name of Jesus.
9. Every inherited limitation, get out of my life now, in Jesus' name.
10. Holy Ghost fire, sanitize my life.
11. (Lay your hands on your head and stomach, and pray thus.) Every sickness in my body, go back to your sender, in the name of Jesus.
12. Every problem in any department of my life, depart, in the name of Jesus.
13. Let the healing power of-God begin to flow into every part of my body and send out every spirit of death, in Jesus' name.
14. Every friend of darkness in my family, be exposed, in Jesus' name.
15. Every satanic coffin constructed for me, fall down and die, in the name of Jesus.
16. Every hindrance against my goal, fall down and die, in Jesus' name.
17. Ask the Lord for supernatural breakthroughs.

# 6
# VAGABOND SPIRITS

## INTRODUCTION

These are spirits responsible for making one a fugitive, wandering, from place to place, without a fixed course. They are responsible for lack of ability to discover oneself. People who are under their attack always fail to find favour with people; their finances are under the firm grip of the extortioner.

## PRAISE WORSHIP

## PRAYER WARFARE

1. Every bitter water flowing into my life, dry up, in Jesus' name.
2. Every satanic prediction and expectation for my life, die, in the name of Jesus.
3. O heavens, declare the glory of God in my life, in Jesus' name.
4. If I am my own problem, deliver me now by Your mercy, O Lord, in the name of Jesus.
5. Every witchcraft bird flying against me, will not return alive, in the name of Jesus.
6. My brain, become a generator of prosperity, in Jesus' name.
7. I receive the baptism of favour, in the name of Jesus.
8. Thou yoke of Kadesh-Barnea, be broken in my life, in Jesus' name.
9. Every vehicle of stagnancy, I kill you today, in Jesus' name.

10. Every stronghold binding me with stagnancy, die, in Jesus' name.
11. Thou power of failure, frustration and backwardness, die, in the name of Jesus.
12. Power to find my bearing in the journey of life, fall upon me now, in the name of Jesus.
13. Thou desert arrows fired into my destiny, backfire, in the name of Jesus.
14. I shall fulfil my destiny at the appointed time, in Jesus' name.
15. My Father, instruct and teach me in the way I should go, in the name of Jesus.
16. I withdraw my name from the book of born-for-nothing, in the name of Jesus.
17. Holy Spirit, cut every umbilical cord still attached to Satan, in the name of Jesus.
18. Every bondage of circular spirits, break, in Jesus' name.
19. Every satanic agenda for my progress, die, in Jesus' name.
20. Every witchcraft legislation against my advancement, die, in the name of Jesus.
21. Every power prolonging my stay in the wilderness, die, in the name of Jesus.
22. I shall not journey for too long before getting to my inheritance., in the name of Jesus.
23. The Lord will make a straight path for my feet and establish my goings this year, in the name of Jesus.
24. I raise the standard of the blood of Jesus against every spirit of Kadesh Barnea in my life, in the name of Jesus.

25. Thou chain of darkness holding me down in the same spot for years, die, in the name of Jesus.
26. I bury every failure, frustration, backwardness and sickness, in the name of Jesus.
27. Thou power of failure at the edge of success, die, in Jesus' name.
28. Every satanic eye monitoring my success and progress, receive blindness, in the name of Jesus.
29. Every gathering against my success, scatter by fire, in the name of Jesus.
30. Every mark of failure at the edge of success, be wiped off by the blood of Jesus.

# 7

# EVIL OBSERVERS

## INTRODUCTION

These are monitoring powers who report people's operations to the dark world. Sometimes they use demonic watchers to keep their victims under observation. Victims of evil observers sometimes have the feelings that they are being watched. Such persons may hear strange voices and sounds which others do not hear. They may discover that there are moving objects in their bodies that cause them discomfort. Such programmed materials, are used as tracers to locate the whereabouts of their victims. It does not matter where they are in the world, evil pursuing powers are able to locate them quite easily.

## PRAISE WORSHIP

## PRAYER WARFARE

1. I release blindness and confusion on every evil observer, in the name of Jesus.
2. Holy Ghost fire, arise in your mighty burning power and destroy all eyes of darkness assigned against me, in the name of Jesus.

3. I release panic upon my full-time enemies, in Jesus' name.
4. Let stubborn confusion come upon the headquarters of my enemies, in the name of Jesus.
5. I release confusion upon the plans of my enemies, in Jesus' name
6. Every stronghold of darkness, receive acidic confusion, in the name of Jesus.
7. I release panic and frustration on satanic orders issued against me, in the name of Jesus.
8. Evil plans against my life, receive confusion, in Jesus' name.
9. All curses and demons programmed against me, I neutralise your power with the blood of Jesus.
10. Every warfare prepared for my peace, I command panic upon you, in the name of Jesus.
11. Every warfare prepared for my peace, I command havoc upon you, in the name of Jesus.
12. Every warfare prepared for my peace, I command chaos upon you, in the name of Jesus.
13. Every warfare prepared for my peace, I command pandemonium upon you, in the name of Jesus.
14. Every warfare prepared for my peace, I command disaster upon you, in the name of Jesus,
15. Every warfare prepared for my peace, I command confusion upon you, in the name of Jesus.
16. Every warfare prepared for my peace, I command spiritual acid upon you, in the name of Jesus.
17. Every warfare prepared for my peace, I command destruction

upon you, in Jesus' name.

18. Every warfare prepared for my peace, I command hornets of the Lord upon you, in the name of Jesus.

19. Every warfare prepared for my peace, I command brimstone and hailstone upon you, in the name of Jesus.

20. I frustrate every satanic verdict issued against me, in Jesus' name.

21. Let the finger, vengeance, terror, anger, fear, wrath, hatred and burning judgement of God be released upon my full-time enemies, in the name of Jesus.

22. Every power preventing the perfect will of God from being done in my life, receive failure and defeat, in Jesus' name.

23. Let the warring angels and the Spirit of God arise and scatter every evil gathering sponsored against me, in Jesus' name.

24. I disobey any satanic order programmed by inheritance unto my life, in the name of Jesus.

25. I bind and cast out every power causing internal warfare, in the name of Jesus.

26. Every demonic doorkeeper locking out good things against me, be paralysed by fire, in the name of Jesus.

27. I command every evil power fighting against me to fight against and destroy one another, in the name of Jesus.

28. Every demon hindering, delaying, preventing, or destroying breakthroughs, receive confusion, in Jesus' name.

29. Let divine power and control attack the spirits of violence and torture, in the name of Jesus.

30. Let the spirit of witchcraft attack familiar spirits fashioned against me, in the name of Jesus.

31. Civil war, occur in the kingdom of darkness, in Jesus' name.

32. Lord, loose judgment and destruction upon all stubborn spirits that fail to follow my commands promptly.

# 8

# SATANIC ARROWS

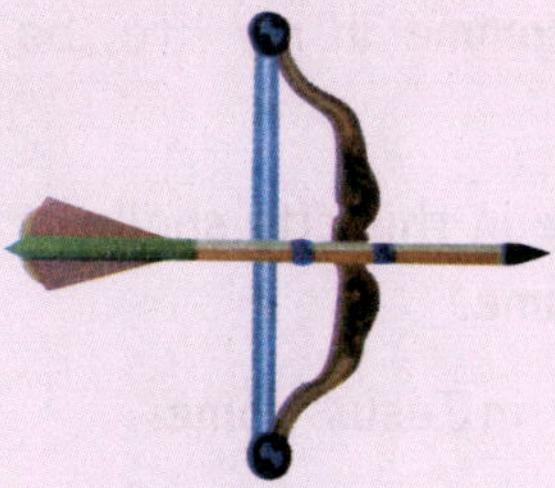

## INTRODUCTION

The Bible talks about the arrows that flieth. There are weapons in the satanic armoury used to torment and destroy. The enemy fires fiery darts at man. The arrows bring sicknesses, failure, backsliding, fear, demotion, death and destruction. Unfortunately, many people have become arrow incubators.

## PRAISE WORSHIP

## CONFESSION

**Numbers 2318:** How shall I curse, whom God hath not cursed? or how shall I def, whom the Lord hath not defied?

## PRAYER WARFARE

1. My place of birth will not be my caldron, in Jesus' name.
2. This city I live in, will not be my caldron, in Jesus' name.
3. Every pot of darkness energised against my life, be destroyed by fire, in the name of Jesus.
4. I command every witchcraft pot, using remote control against my health to be broken into pieces, in Jesus' name.
5. Every power calling my name into any caldron, fall down and die, in the name of Jesus.
6. Every caldron making noise against me and monitoring my life, disintegrate, in the name of Jesus.

7. Every power cooking my progress in an evil pot, receive the fire of judgment, in the name of Jesus.

8. Every satanic programme emanating from the caldron of darkness, be reversed, in the name of Jesus.

9. Any evil fire fuelling any satanic programme in my life, be quenched, in the name of Jesus.

10, The counsel of the wicked against my life in this city shall not stand. I command it to perish, in Jesus' name.

11, Let the counsel of God for my life prosper, in Jesus' name.

12. Every power cooking my flesh and my health in any evil caldron, receive the fire of God, in the name of Jesus.

13. Every evil bird of satanic programme emanating from any caldron of darkness, fall down and die, in Jesus' name.

14. Every pot cooking my affairs, the Lord rebuke you, in Jesus' name.

15. I rebuke the spell of any witchcraft pot, in Jesus' name.

16. I break every witchcraft pot over my life, in Jesus' name.

17. Let every evil pot hunt its owners, in the name of Jesus.

18. Every evil caldron or pot, be judged from heaven, in Jesus' name.

19. No evil caldron will cook up my life, in the name of Jesus.

20. Every council of witchcraft working against me will not prosper, in the name of Jesus.

21. Every agreement with Satan over my life, I cancel you now, in Jesus' name.

22. Every astral projection against me, I frustrate you, in Jesus' name.

23. I disentangle myself and my family from every witchcraft cage and pot, in the name of Jesus.
24. Every enemy that will not let me go easily, I bring the judgment of death against you, in Jesus' name.
25. This year, my blessings will not sink, in the name of Jesus.
26. Let the spirit of salvation fall upon my family, in Jesus' name.
27. Every grip, of the evil consequences of the ancestral worship of my forefathers' god over my life and ministry, break by fire, in Jesus' name.
28. Every covenant with water spirits, desert spirits, witchcraft spirits, spirits in evil sacred trees, spirits inside / under sacred rocks / hills, family gods, evil family guardian spirits, family / village serpentine spirits, masquerade spirits, and inherited spirit husbands / wives, be broken by the blood of Jesus.
29. Every unconscious evil soul-tie and covenant with the spirits of my dead grandfather, grandmother, occult uncles, aunties, custodian of family gods/oracles/shrines, be broken by the blood of Jesus.
30. Every decision, vow or promise made by my forefathers contrary to my divine destiny, loose your hold by fire, in the name of Jesus.
31. Every legal ground that ancestral/guardian spirits have in my life, be destroyed by the blood of Jesus.
32. Every generational curse of God resulting from the sin of idolatry on my forefathers, loose your hold, in Jesus' name.
33. Every ancestral evil altar prospering against me, be dashed against the Rock of Ages, in the name of Jesus.
34. Every ancestral placenta manipulation of my life, be reversed, in

the name of Jesus.

35. Every evil ancestral life pattern designed for me through vows. promises and covenants, be reversed, in Jesus' name.

36. Every hold of any sacrifice ever offered in my family or behalf, I break your power over my life, in Jesus' name.

37. Any ancestral bloodshed of animals or human beings affecting me, loose your hold by the blood of Jesus.

38. Any curse placed on my ancestral line by anybody cheated, maltreated or at the point of death, break now, in Jesus' name.

39. Every garment of ancestral infirmity, disease, sickness, untimely death, poverty, disfavour, dishonour, shame and failure at the edge of miracles, passed down to my generation, be roasted by fire, in the name of Jesus.

40. Every evil ancestral river flowing down to my generation, I cut you off, in the name of Jesus.

41, Every evil ancestral habit and weakness of morals manifesting in my life, loose your grip and release me now, in Jesus' name.

42. Any power from my family background seeking to make shipwreck of my life and ministry, be destroyed by the fire of God, in the name of Jesus.

43. Every rage and rampage of ancestral and family spirits resulting from my being born again, be quenched by the liquid fire of God, in Jesus' name.

44. Any ancestral power frustrating any area of my life to discourage me from following Christ, receive multiple destruction, in the name of Jesus.

45. Every ancestral chain of slavery binding my people from

prospering in life, you are broken in my life by the hammer of God, in the name of Jesus.

46. The height nobody has attained in my generation, I will reach, in Jesus' name.

47. I recover every good thing stolen by ancestral evil spirits from my forefathers, my immediate family and myself, in Jesus' name.

48. Every ancestral embargo, be lifted; and let good things begin to break forth in my life and in my family, in Jesus' name.

49. I release myself from any inherited bondage, in Jesus' name.

50. O Lord, send Your axe of fire to the foundation of my life and destroy every evil plantation there.

51. Let the blood of Jesus flush out from my system every inherited satanic deposit, in Jesus' name.

52. I release myself from the grip of any problem transferred into my life from the womb, in Jesus' name.

53. I break and loose myself from every inherited evil covenant, in Jesus' name.

54. I break and loose myself from every inherited evil curse, in Jesus' name.

55. I vomit every evil thing that I have been fed with as a child, in the name of Jesus.

56. I command all foundational strongmen attached to my life to be paralysed, in the name of Jesus.

57. Let any rod of the wicked rising up against my family line, be rendered impotent for my sake, in the name of Jesus.

58. I cancel all the consequences of any evil local name attached to

me, in the name of Jesus.

59. You evil foundational plantations, come out of my life with all your roots, in the name of Jesus.

60. I break and loose myself from every form of demonic bewitchment, in the name of Jesus.

61. I release myself from every evil domination and control, in Jesus' name.

62. Let every gate opened to the enemy by my foundation, be closed forever with the blood of Jesus,

63. Lord Jesus, walk back into every second of my life, and deliver me where I need deliverance, heal me where I need healing, transform me where I need transformation.

64. Let every evil imagination against me, wither from the source, in the name of Jesus.

65. All those laughing me to scorn, shall witness my testimony, in Jesus' name.

66. Let all the destructive plans of the enemies aimed at me blow up in their faces, in Jesus' name.

67. Let my point of ridicule be converted to a source of miracles, in Jesus' name.

68. Let all powers sponsoring evil decisions against me be disgraced, in the name of Jesus.

69. Let the stubborn strongman commissioned against me, fall down to the ground and become impotent, in Jesus' name.

70. Let the stronghold of every spirit of Korah, Dathan and Abiram militating against me, be smashed to pieces, in the name of Jesus.

71. Let every spirit of Balaam hired to curse me, fall after the order of Balaam, in the name of Jesus.

72. Let every spirit of Sanballat and Tobiah planning evil against me receive the stones of fire, in the name of Jesus.

73. Let every spirit of Egypt, fall after the order of Pharaoh, in Jesus' name.

74. Let every spirit of Herod be disgraced, in Jesus' name.

75. Let every spirit of Goliath receive the stones of fire, in Jesus' name.

76. Let every spirit of Pharaoh fall into the Red Sea of its own creation, in the name of Jesus.

77. Let all satanic manipulations aimed at changing my destiny be frustrated, in the name of Jesus.

78. Let all evil broad casters of my goodness be silenced, in the name of Jesus.

79. Let all leaking bags and pockets be sealed up, in Jesus' name.

80. Let all evil monitoring eyes fashioned against me become blind, in Jesus' name.

81. Let every evil effect of any strange touch be removed from my life, in the name of Jesus.

82. I command all demonic reverse gears installed to hinder my progress to be roasted, in Jesus' name.

83. Any evil sleep undertaken to harm me, be converted to death sleep, in the name of Jesus.

84. Let all weapons and devices of the oppressors and tormentors be rendered impotent, in Jesus' name.

85. Let the fire of God destroy every power operating any spiritual vehicle working against me, in the name of Jesus.

86. Let all evil advice given against my favour crash and disintegrate, in the name of Jesus.

87. Let the wind, the sun and the moon run contrary to every demonic presence in my environment, in the name of Jesus.

88. O you devourers, vanish from my labour, in Jesus' name.

89. Let every tree planted by fear in my life dry up from the roots, in the name of Jesus.

90. I cancel all the enchantments, curses and spells that are against me, in the name of Jesus.

91. Let all iron-like curses break, in the name of Jesus.

92. Let divine tongues of fire roast any evil tongue that is against me, in the name of Jesus.

93. Lord, I thank You very much for everything You have done for me through these prayer points.

# 9

# DESERT SPIRITS

## INTRODUCTION

In the desert, there is absence of vegetation, life, water and leisure. It is a punishing environment and a dry place. Desert spirits are spirits responsible for physical and spiritual dryness, abject poverty and general stagnancy. The invasion of any life by these spirits, leads to tragedy including suicidal tendencies and the conversion of one's prosperity to poverty.

## PRAISE WORSHIP

## PRAYER WARFARE

1. I release myself from the grip and power of the wasters, in the name of Jesus.
2. Let every power of unfruitfulness disappear from my handiwork, in the name of Jesus.
3. Holy Spirit, pour Your soothing oil upon every dry area of my life, in the name of Jesus.
4. Every desert serpent and scorpion militating against my breakthroughs, I bury you today, in the name of Jesus.
5. I command complete deliverance upon my brain, in Jesus' name. Thou power of cobweb spirits, I bind and cast you out of my life., in the name of Jesus.
7. Every dry bone of my destiny caged in the wilderness of

witchcraft, receive life, in the name of Jesus.

8. Thou power of resurrection of the Lord Jesus Christ, incubate every area of my destiny, in the name of Jesus.
9. The oppressor and tormentor will no longer have access to my destiny, in the name of Jesus.
10. Let the fire of God burn to ashes, every handwriting of unfruitfulness, in the name of Jesus.
11. Every power swallowing up my words, die, in Jesus' name.
12. Every yoke of desert spirit, break, in the name of Jesus.
13. Spirit of the living God, move upon my destiny in a new way, in the name of Jesus.
14. O God that answers by fire, disgrace every enchantment and incantation issued against my progress, in Jesus' name.
15. Let my land become a land of miracles and power, in Jesus' name.
16. Whenever I walk in, let darkness walk out, in Jesus' name.
17. I refuse to be a student in the school of failure, in Jesus' name.
18. By the thunder of Your power, bulldoze every hindrance away from my promised land, in the name of Jesus,
19. I will move forward and rise above all the unbelievers around me, in the name of Jesus.
20 Let Your hand cause my life to blossom, in Jesus' name.
21. Holy Ghost, move me forward by Your power, in Jesus' name.
22. Every power that wants to detain me in the desert of destruction, loose your hold, in the name of Jesus.
23. Every power of the mistress of witchcraft upon my life, I bury you today, in the name of Jesus.

24. Let my destiny move forward in a way that will shock and surprise my enemies, in the name of Jesus.

25. Every weapon of wastage fashioned against me, be destroyed, in the name of Jesus.

26. My life will be an example of the manifestation of divine power, in the name of Jesus.

27. Holy Ghost and fire, disgrace every power that wants to disgrace me, in the name of Jesus.

28. Every curse of dryness targeted against me, blood of Jesus, wipe it off.

# 10

# EVIL MARKERS

## INTRODUCTION

These are spirits that mark people out for destruction. For their marks, they use invisible satanic ink which makes it easy to identify and locate their victims. These marks can be recognized by occultists and evil observers. Geographical location does not constitute an immunity to being identified with the evil marks. See Ezekiel chapter 9.

**PRAISE WORSHIP**

**PRAYER WARFARE**

1. I bury every power that wants to bury me alive, in Jesus' name.
2. I command disgrace upon every power marking me out for attacks, in the name of Jesus.
3. Every unconscious or conscious evil mark, be wiped off by the blood of Jesus.
4. Every mark of demotion, be wiped off by the blood of Jesus.
5. Every mark of lost opportunity, be wiped off by the blood of Jesus.
6. Every mark of untimely death, be wiped off by the blood of Jesus.
7. Every mark of backwardness, be wiped off by the blood of Jesus.
8. Every mark of lukewarmness, be wiped off by the blood of Jesus.
9. Every mark of marital failure, be wiped off by the blood of Jesus.

10. Every mark of distress, be wiped off by the blood of Jesus.
11. Every mark of infirmity, be wiped off by the blood of Jesus.
12. Every mark of dream attack, be wiped off by the blood of Jesus.
13. Every mark of evil accusation, be wiped off by the blood of Jesus.
14. Every mark of torment, be wiped off by the blood of Jesus.
15. Every mark of affliction, be wiped off by the blood of Jesus.
16. Every mark of failure at the edge of success, be wiped off by the blood of Jesus.
17. Every mark of aimlessness, be wiped off by the blood of Jesus.
18. Every mark of confusion, be wiped off by the blood of Jesus.
19. Every mark of poverty, be wiped off by the blood of Jesus.
20. Every mark of backsliding, be wiped off by the blood of Jesus.
21. Every mark of demonic delay, be wiped off by the blood of Jesus.
22. Every monitoring power, receive blindness, in Jesus' name.
23. Every harassment of the enemy, go back to your sender, in the name of Jesus.
24. Any power in the garden of my life working against my promotion, I destroy you now, in the name of Jesus.
25. I shall be the head and not the tail, in the name of Jesus.
26. Every power that has marked me down for attacks, be frustrated, in the name of Jesus.
27. Every imagination of destruction against me, vanish, in the name of Jesus.
28. I shall mount up with wings as eagles, and I shall be a strong arrow in the hands of my God, in the name of Jesus.

# 11

# BUSINESS BEWITCHERS

## INTRODUCTION

These are spirits that plague businesses with profitless investments, unexplainable losses, 'rat workers, unprofitable business locations, financial insolvency and loss of customers.

## PRAISE WORSHIP

## PRAYER WARFARE

1. I refuse every spiritual demotion, in the name of Jesus.
2. Every strange fire prepared against my prosperity, be quenched, in the name of Jesus.
3. Every power sending my money to a spiritual mortuary, fall down and die, in the name of Jesus
4. Every power scaring away my prosperity, be paralysed, in the name of Jesus.
5. Every familiar spirit spending my money before I receive it, be bound, in the name of Jesus.
6. Every evil ugly foot, walk out of my life, in Jesus' name.
7. Every satanic re-arrangement of my prosperity, be dismantled, in the name of Jesus
8. O Lord, lead me to my own promised land that flows with milk and

honey, in the name of Jesus.

9. Every satanic giant occupying my promised land, fall down and die, in the name of Jesus
10. Anybody wickedly sitting on my money, be gored with the sword of fire, in the name of Jesus.
11. O Lord, empower me to climb the mountain of prosperity, in the name of Jesus.
12. You strongman of poverty, fall down and die with your rags, in the name of Jesus,
13. You the spirit of famine and hunger, my life is not for you, in the name of Jesus.
14. I remove my name from the book of financial embarrassment, in the name of Jesus.
15. Every power reinforcing poverty in my life, loose your hold, in the name of Jesus.
16. O Lord, make me a reference point of divine prosperity, in the name of Jesus.
17. I receive the anointing of excellence, in the name of Jesus.
18. O Lord, let harvest meet harvest in my life, in Jesus' name
19. O Lord, let my harvest overtake the sower, in Jesus' name.
20. I reject every financial burial, in the name of Jesus.
21. I reject witchcraft burial of my money, in Jesus' name.
22. Every stolen and satanically transferred virtue from my life, be restored, in the name of Jesus.
23. O Lord, create new and profitable opportunities for me, in the name of Jesus.

# 12

# MARRIAGE KILLERS

## INTRODUCTION

These are spirits of marriage destruction. They initiate and sponsor family strife, infidelity, divorce, marriage breakdown and general marital distress.

### PRAISE WORSHIP

### PRAYER WARFARE

1. You, who conspired with my husband/wife to destroy our marriage and good home, I command you to remove your hands from my husband/wife, in the name of Jesus. It is against God''s word for you to separate us.
2. All evil counsels against our home, collapse, in Jesus' name.
3. I scatter all arrangements between you and my husband/wife, in the name of Jesus.
4. Dislike one another as from now, in the name of Jesus.
5. I will get the favour and love of my husband/wife, in Jesus' name.
6. Thank the Lord for His mercies and grace.
7. Ask the Holy Spirit to help you pray to the point of breakthrough.

8. *(Gird up your spiritual loins and aggressively stand against the following local home-wreckers. Pray as follows:)* I stand against any..., (fix in the items listed hereunder) and command it/them to release you and your marriage, in the name of Jesus.

   (a) Competition by strange women or girls\men

   (b) Demonic in-laws

   (c) Financial failure and poverty, especially after the wedding

   (d) Spirit husbands and wives

   (e) Demonic marks

   (f) Marriage destruction

   (g) Spirit of fear

   (h) Spirit of Jezebel (domineering nature)

   (i) Inherited spirit from the father's and mother's sides

   (j) Marriage curses

   (k) Evil marriage covenants

   (l) Spirit of misunderstanding, misinterpretation and exaggeration

   (m) Ungodly attachment to parents.

9. *(Cancel the effects of the following things. Please, pray aggressively if you are involved in them. Pray as follows:)* I cancel the satanic influence of . . . upon my marriage: I bind the connected spirits and command them to loose their hold upon my marriage, in the name of Jesus.

   (a) Demonic water-pouring on the feet on the wedding day

   (b) Contaminated wedding rings and shoes

   (c) Background of polygamy and multiple husbands/wives

   (d) Familiar spirits and witchcraft spirits

   (e) Satanic deposits in the home

   (f) Collection of spiritual bride-price

(g) Incest.

10. I break and loose myself, in the name of Jesus, from any anti. marriage curse issued upon my family.

11. Father, let the Prince of Peace reign in my marriage without any hindrance, in Jesus' name.

12. I decree reconciliation between myself and my partner, in the name of Jesus.

13 All powers conspiring with anyone to destroy our home \marriage loose your hold, in the name of Jesus.

14. All evil counsels against our home, be frustrated, in Jesus' name.

## 13

# SPIRITUAL MARRIAGE

### INTRODUCTION

These are vicious sexual spirits which can molest and torment susceptible victims. Sexual spirits that attack women are called incubus and those who violate men are called succubus. The problem of spiritual marriage is one of the greatest problems, which has pervaded all societies of the world. Once a spiritual marriage is in place, evil forces will neutralise your prayers on legal grounds. Evil spiritual marriage has the power to control, rule, dominate, abuse, manipulate, plunder and dispossess one of every good thing earmarked for him by God.

The chief purpose of a spiritual marriage is to convert one's life to a dustbin or a garbage dump. By its activities, one's marital, social, business, financial and spiritual life would be in shambles.

**PRAISE WORSHIP**

**PRAYER WARFARE**

**Make the following confessions:**

*In the beginning God created man to subdue the earth and have dominion over all the fishes of the sea, and over all the fowls of the air and over every creature that moveth upon the face of the earth. The psalmist confirms this, as he writes that God has made man have dominion over all the works of His hands: Thou hath put all things under his feet. All sheep and oxen, the beasts of the field, the fowls of the air, and the fishes of the sea and whatsoever passeth through the PA THS OF THE SEAS.*

*The mandate every man lost to the devil through Adam's disobedience, has been restored unto us by Jesus Christ. I am a workmanship of God, recreated in Christ as a priest and king to reign here on earth.*

*Jesus Christ was made manifest, that He might destroy all the works of the devil. When He was going, He said that greater works than He did, I shall do.*

*Therefore as I go into this prayer, I hold in my hand the victory Jesus Christ purchased on the cross at calvary, when He made an open show of principalities and powers. I take my position in Christ as one given power to become a son of God, even a joint heir of the kingdom of God with Christ, to execute judgment against every form of disobedience exhibited against the knowledge of God.*

*Greater is He that is in me, than any power on earth and in the seas. I am born of God, and I have overcome the world with my faith.*

*By faith, I hand over my battle to God. By faith, I come against evil strongholds of any marine kingdom. By faith, I pollute their water with the blood of Jesus Christ. By faith, I dethrone every queen enthroned against me. By faith, I trample upon her serpents and scorpions. By faith I destroy her palace and set her captives free.*

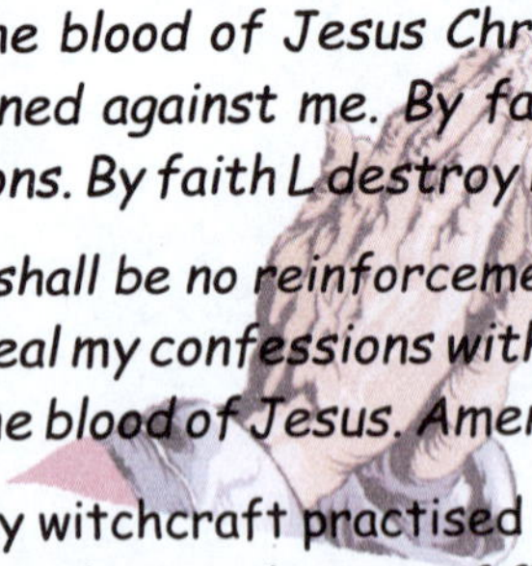

*There shall be no reinforcement or evil reunion of this power against me. I seal my confessions with the blood of Jesus and I cover myself with the blood of Jesus. Amen.*

1. Any witchcraft practised under any water against my life, receive immediate judgment of fire, in the name of Jesus.
2. Let every evil altar under any water upon which certain evils are

done against me, be roasted, in the name of Jesus.

3. Every priest ministering on any evil altar inside any water against me, fall down and die, in the name of Jesus.

4. Any power under any river or sea remotely-controlling my life, be destroyed by fire, and I shake myself loose from your hold, in the name of Jesus.

5. Let any evil monitoring mirror ever used against me under any water, break to irredeemable pieces, in Jesus' name.

6. Every marine witchcraft that has introduced spirit husband/wife or child into my dreams, be roasted by fire, in Jesus' name.

7. Every agent of marine witchcraft posing as my husband, wife or child in my dreams, be roasted by fire, in Jesus' name.

8. Every agent of marine witchcraft physically attached to my marriage to frustrate it, fall down and perish now, in Jesus' name.

9. Every agent of marine witchcraft assigned to attack my finances through dream-attacks, fall down and perish, in Jesus' name.

10. I pull down every stronghold of bewitchment, enchantment, jinx, divination, fashioned against me by marine witches, in Jesus' name.

11. Let the thunderbolt of God, locate and destroy every marine witchcraft coven, where deliberations and decisions have ever been fashioned against me, in Jesus' name.

12. Any water spirit from my village, or the place of my birth, practising witchcraft against me and my family, be amputated by the word of God, in Jesus' name.

13. Let every spiritual weapon of wickedness fashioned against me under any river or sea, be roasted by the fire of God, in the name

of Jesus.

14. Any power of marine witchcraft holding any of my blessings in bondage, receive the fire of God and release them. in Jesus name.
15. I loose my mind and soul from the bondage of marine witches, in the name of Jesus.
16. Any marine witchcraft chain, hindering my hands and feet from prospering, be shattered to pieces, in Jesus' name.
17. Every arrow shot into my life from under any water through witchcraft, come out of me and go back to your sender, in the name of Jesus.
18. Any evil material transferred into my body through contact with any marine witchcraft agent, be roasted by fire, in Jesus' name.
19. Every sexual pollution of marine spirit husband/wife in my body, be flushed out by the blood of Jesus.
20. Any evil name given to me under any water, I reject and cancel it with the blood of Jesus.
21. Every image constructed under any water to manipulate me, be roasted by fire, in the name of Jesus.
22. Any evil done against me so far through marine witchcraft, oppression and manipulation, be reversed by the blood of Jesus.
23. Spirit husband/spirit wife, release me by fire, in Jesus' name.
24. Every spirit husband/wife, I divorce you by the blood of Jesus.
25. Every spirit husband/wife, die, in Jesus' name.
26. Everything you have deposited in my life, come out by fire, in Jesus' name.

27. Every power that is working against my marriage, fall down and die, in the name of Jesus.

28. I divorce and renounce my marriage with the spirit husband/wife, in the name of Jesus.

29. I break all covenants entered into with spirit husband/wife, in the name of Jesus.

30. I command the thunder fire of God to burn to ashes, the wedding gown, ring. photographs and all other materials used for spiritual marriage, in Jesus' name.

31. I send the fire of God to burn to ashes the marriage certificate, in the name of Jesus.

32. I break every blood and soul-tie covenant with the spirit husband/wife, in the name of Jesus.

33. I send the thunder fire of God to burn to ashes, the children born to the marriage, in Jesus' name.

34. I withdraw my blood, sperm or any other thing from my body deposited in the altar of the spirit husband/wife, in Jesus' name.

35. You spirit husband or wife tormenting my life and physical marriage, I bind you with hot chains and fetters of God and cast you out of my life into the deep pit, and I command you never to come into my life again, in the name of Jesus.

36. I return to you every property of yours in my possession in the spirit world, including the bride price and whatsoever was used for the marriage and covenants, in Jesus' name.

37. I drain myself of all evil materials deposited in my body as a result of our sexual relations, in the name of Jesus.

38. Lord, send Holy Ghost fire into my root. and burn out all unclean

things deposited in it by the spirit husband/wife, in Jesus' name.

39. I break the head of the snake deposited in my body by the spirit husband or wife to do me harm, and command it to come out, in the name of Jesus.

40. I purge myself with the blood of Jesus, every evil material deposited in my womb to prevent me from having children on earth.

41. Lord, repair and restore every damage done to any part of my body and my physical marriage by the spirit husband/wife, in the name of Jesus.

42. I reject and cancel every curse, evil pronouncement, spell, jinx, enchantment and incantation placed upon me by the spirit husband/wife, in the name of Jesus.

43. I take back and possess all my physical belongings in the custody of the spirit husband/wife, in the name of Jesus.

44. I command the spirit husband/wife to turn his or her back on me forever, in Jesus' name.

45. I renounce and reject the name given to me by the spirit husband or wife, in the name of Jesus.

46. I hereby declare and confess that the Lord Jesus Christ is my Husband for eternity, in Jesus' name.

47 I soak myself in the blood of Jesus and cancel the evil mark placed on me, in Jesus' name.

48 I set myself free from the stronghold and domineering power and bondage of the spirit husband/wife, in the name of Jesus.

49. I paralyse the remote controlling power and work used to destabilise my physical marriage and to hinder my having children

on earth, in the name of Jesus.

50. I announce to the heavens that I am married forever to Jesus.
51. Every trademark of evil marriage, be shaken out of my life, in Jesus' name.
52. Every evil mark engraved with an iron pen, be wiped off by the blood of Jesus.
53. I bring the blood of Jesus upon the spirit that does not want to go, in the name of Jesus.
54. I bring the blood of Jesus on every evidence that can be tendered by wicked spirits against.
55. I file a counter-report in the heavens against every evil marriage, in the name of Jesus.
56. I refuse to supply any evidence that the enemy may use against me, in the name of Jesus.
57. Let satanic exhibitions be destroyed by the blood of Jesus.
58. I declare to you, spirit husband/wife that there is no vacancy for you in my life, in the name of Jesus.
59, O Lord, make me a vehicle of deliverance.
60. I come by faith to mount Zion, Lord, command deliverance upon my life now.
61. Lord, water me from the waters of God.
62. Let the carefully planned siege of the enemy for my life be dismantled, in Jesus' name.
63. O Lord, defend Your interest in my life.
64. Everything written in the cycle of the moon, be blotted out, in the name of Jesus.

65. Everything programmed into the sun, moon and stars against me, be dismantled, in Jesus' name.
66. Every evil thing programmed into my genes, be blotted out by the blood of Jesus.
67. O Lord, shake out seasons of failure and frustration from my life.
68. I overthrow every wicked law working against my life, in Jesus' name.
69. I ordain a new time, season and profitable law, in Jesus' name.
70. I speak destruction unto the palaces of the queen of the coast and of the rivers, in Jesus' name.
71. I speak destruction unto the headquarters of the spirit of Egypt and blow up their altars, in the name of Jesus.
72. I speak destruction unto the altars speaking against the purpose of God for my life, in the name of Jesus.
73. I declare myself a virgin for the Lord, in Jesus' name.
74. Let every evil veil upon my life be shredded, in Jesus' name.
75. Every wall between me and the visitation of God, be broken, in Jesus' name.
76. Let the counsel of God prosper in my life, in Jesus' name.
77. I destroy the power of any demonic seed in my life from the womb, in the name of Jesus.
78. I speak unto my umbilical gate to overthrow all negative parental spirits, in the name of Jesus.
79. I break the yoke of the spirits having access to my reproductive

80. O Lord, let Your time of refreshing come upon me.

81. I bring fire from the altar of the Lord upon every evil marriage, in the name of Jesus.

82. I redeem myself from every sex trap by the blood of Jesus, in Jesus' name.

83. I erase the engraving of my name, on any evil marriage record, in the name of Jesus.

84. I reject and renounce, every evil spiritual marriage, in Jesus' name.

85. I confess that Jesus is my original spouse and is jealous over me.

86. I issue a bill of divorce to every spirit husband/wife, in Jesus' name.

87. I bind every spirit husband/wife with everlasting chains, in Jesus' name.

88. Let heavenly testimony overcome every evil testimony of hell, in Jesus' name.

89. O Lord, bring to my remembrance every spiritual trap and contract.

90. Let the blood of Jesus purge me of every contaminating material, in the name of Jesus.

91, Let the spirit husband/wife fall down and die, in Jesus' name.

92. Let all the children attached to me by the spirit husband/wife fall down and die, in the name of Jesus.

93. I burn the certificates and destroy the rings of the spirit husband/wife, in Jesus' name.

94. I execute judgement against water spirits and declare that they

are reserved for everlasting chains of darkness, in Jesus' name

95. O Lord, contend with those who are contending with me.

96. Every trademark of the water spirit, be shaken out of my life, in Jesus' name.

72. Thank God for your deliverance.

# 14

# ARROWS OF INFIRMITY

## INTRODUCTION

The Bible talks about the arrows that fly by noonday and the fiery darts of the enemy. Arrows of infirmity are spiritual missiles fired to initiate or prolong infirmities or diseases. These arrows sometimes act as forerunners of the spirit of death and hell.

## PRAISE WORSHIP

## PRAYER WARFARE

1. The sun will not smite me by day, nor the moon by night, in the name of Jesus.
2. Every arrow of infirmity, depart from my life and go back to your sender, in the name of Jesus.
3. Holy Ghost fire, eject from my body every arrow of infirmity, in the name of Jesus.
4. Let my rain of abundant health begin to fall, in Jesus' name.
5. I depart from the school of infirmity by fire, in Jesus' name.
6. Holy Ghost, plug my body into the socket of divine health, in the name of Jesus.
7. Healing winds of God, blow upon all the organs of my body, in the name of Jesus.

8. O God arise, and withdraw my organs from every satanic altar, in the name of Jesus.

9 Fire of God, boil infirmities out of my blood, in Jesus' name.

10. Thou creative power of God, work upon my lite, in Jesus' name

11. Glory of God, overshadow my body, soul and spirit, in Jesus' name

12. Create new organs to replace sick or dead ones in my body, o Lord, in the name of Jesus.

13. O God, supply organ spare parts to my body, in Jesus' name.

14. Heavenly Surgeon, visit me now, in the name of Jesus.

15. Power of God, pull down every stronghold of stubborn infirmities, in the name of Jesus.

16. Fire of God, purge my organs and make them new, in Jesus' name.

17. Let my youth be renewed as the eagles, in Jesus' name.

18. Every handwriting of darkness targeted at my health, be wiped off, in the name of Jesus.

19. My organs, receive creative miracles, in the name of Jesus.

20. Spirit of God, move upon every organ in my body, in Jesus' name.

21, Creative power of God, work in me now, in Jesus' name.

22. I bind every spirit of death operating in my ..., in the mighty name of Jesus.

23. Let Your resurrection power come upon my ..., in Jesus' name.

24. I command every dead bone in my ... to come alive, in the name of Jesus.

25. You evil hand laid on my. . , receive the thunder fire of God and be roasted, in the name of Jesus.

26. I command every evil monitoring gadget fashioned against my.. ..to be destroyed, in the name of Jesus.
27. I breathe in the life of God and I reject every spirit of death and hell, in the name of Jesus.
28. I recover every miracle that I have lost through unbelief, in the name of Jesus.
29. Father, let Your creative power operate afresh in every area of my life, in the name of Jesus.
30. Father, let the fire of the Holy Ghost enter into my blood stream and cleanse my system, in the name of Jesus.
31. I release my......from the cage of every household wickedness, in the name of Jesus.
32. Let every information about my . . . . . be erased from every satanic memory, in the name of Jesus.
33. I command every evil plantation in my life: Come out with all your roots, in the name of Jesus! (Lay your hands on your stomach and keep repeating the emphasized area.)
34. Evil strangers in my body, come all the way out of your hiding places, in the name of Jesus.
35. I cough out and vomit any food eaten from the table of the devil, in the name of Jesus. (Cough it out and vomit it by faith. Prime the expulsion.)
36. Let all negative materials circulating in my blood stream be evacuated, in the name of Jesus.
37. I drink the blood of Jesus. (Physically swallow it by faith. Do this for some time.)

38. Lay one hand on your head and the other on your stomach or navel and pray like this: Holy Ghost fire, burn from the top of my head to the soles of my feet. (Mention every organ of your body: your kidney, liver, intestines, blood, etc. You must not rush at this level, because the fire will actually come and you may start feeling the heat.)

39. I cut myself off every spirit of... (mention the name of your place of birth), in the name of Jesus.

40. I cut myself off every tribal spirit and curse, in Jesus' name.

41. I cut myself off every territorial spirit and curse, in Jesus' name.

42. Holy Ghost fire, purge my life.

43. I claim complete deliverance, in the name of Jesus, from the spirit of...(mention those things you do not desire in your life).

44. I break the hold of any evil power over my life, in Jesus' name.

45. I move from bondage into liberty, in the name of Jesus.

46 Thank God for answers to these prayer points.

# 15

## SHAME DISTRIBUTORS

### INTRODUCTION

These are spirits despatched against people to cause disgrace and dishonour. They did terrible havoc in the lives of Samson and Saul. They initiate situations which result in open disgrace and shame. They are responsible for blinding people, from foreseeing the likely shameful outcome of certain activities. But the word of God says: "For thou will not leave his soul in hell, nor suffer thy Holy One to see corruption."

**PRAISE WORSHIP**

**PRAYER WARFARE**

1. I refuse to be disgraced by any power living or dead, in the name of Jesus.
2. Let divine miracle power overshadow my life, in Jesus' name. name.
3. Every power targeting my life for disgrace, scatter, in the name of Jesus.
4. I shall not see corruption, but I shall see the goodness of the Lord in the land of the living.
5. O God, arise and let all shame distributors scatter, in Jesus' name.
6. Let every yoke of stagnancy and frustration be broken, in the

name of Jesus.

7. I shall arise out of every valley of shame, unto the mountain of elevation and glory, in the name of Jesus.

8. O Lord, plant heavenly deposits into my life that will make me shine, in the name of Jesus.

9. Every satanic rope tying me down to the past, be broken, in the name of Jesus.

10. O arm of the Lord, arise with all Your weapons and defeat defeat in my life, in the name of Jesus.

11. O God arise and make my life to shine above my fellows, in the name of Jesus.

12. O strength of God, empower me, in the name of Jesus.

13. O wisdom of God, instruct me, in the name of Jesus.

14. O light of God, disband my darkness, in the name of Jesus.

15. Every Goliath moving about in the garden of my life, die, in the name of Jesus.

16. Thou power of God, move my life forward speedily, in Jesus' name.

17. I shake off the viper of disgrace into the fire of God, in the name of Jesus.

18. The enemy will not write the last chapter of my life, in the name of Jesus.

19. O God, arise and let every enemy of my progress scatter, in the name of Jesus.

20. My Glory and the Lifter of my head, move me forward by fire, in the name of Jesus.

21. Power to mount up with wings as eagles, come upon my life, in the

name of Jesus.

22. O God, arise and make me a demonstration of what Your power can do, in the name of Jesus.
23. Wherever I walk in, shame and disgrace must walk out, in the name of Jesus.
24. Spirit of the living God, arise by Your fire and disgrace every oppressor, in the name of Jesus.
25. By the thunder of Your power, O God, arise and pursue my pursuers, in the name of Jesus.
26. Let me be a living example of Your power of promotion, in the name of Jesus.
27. Thou power of the grave, release my virtues, in Jesus' name.
28. Every satanic authority in my family line, scatter, in Jesus' name.

# 16

# TERRITORIAL DEMOTERS

## INTRODUCTION

These are environmental demons that arrest the destinies of people living in a particular locality. They work very hard to brutalise, downgrade and demote people within their jurisdiction.

## PRAISE WORSHIP

## PRAYER WARFARE

1. I take authority over every satanic power working against my environmental deliverance, in the name of Jesus.
2. Thou power of God, deliver me from every environmental demotion, in the name of Jesus.
3. Thou controlling power over my environment, I pul you down, in the name of Jesus.
4. Every local prince of Persia controlling my territory, I pull you down, in the name of Jesus.
5. O Lord, let Your angels pursue my pursuers day and night, in the name of Jesus.
6. Every territorial altar ministering against me, be dismantled, in the name of Jesus.

7. I charge my territory with the blood of Jesus, and the fire of the Holy Ghost, in the name of Jesus.
8. Every environmental stronghold and satanic structure, scatter by fire, in the name of Jesus.
9. I take authority over 500 miles radius from where I am, in the name of Jesus.
10. Let the prosperity of territorial powers be turned into poverty, in the name of Jesus.
11. I speak destruction and confusion into the camp of every evil territorial power, in the name of Jesus.
12. Thou power of demotion, go: thou power of promotion, come, in the name of Jesus.
13. My environment, become too hot for territorial demons to occupy, in the name of Jesus.
14. By Your mighty power, O Lord, barricade my life, in Jesus' name.
15. Let my environment refuse to listen to the voice of my enemies, in the name of Jesus.
16. I shall thrive in any environment by the power of the Holy Spirit, in the name of Jesus.
17. I shall be an arrow in the hands of my God, to bring deliverance to His people, in the name of Jesus.
18. Holy Ghost fire, saturate my environment and bring forth testimonies, in the name of Jesus.
19. I bind and cast out every territorial power working against my destiny, in the name of Jesus.
20. I command the queen of heaven over my territory, to crash land,

in the name of Jesus.

21. Any power strengthening territorial powers, loose your hold, in the name of Jesus.
22. Let Your warring angels arise, O Lord, and cleanse my environment with Your fire, in the name of Jesus.
23. I dissociate myself from any evil environmental name, in the name of Jesus.
24. My Father, move by Your military power and capture this environment to the glory of Your name, in Jesus' name.
25. Every satanic check-point in the heavenlies, be bulldozed by the fire of the Holy Ghost, in the name of Jesus.
26. Every evil power sitting upon the throne of my territory, be overthrown, in the name of Jesus.

# 17

# OCCULT ARROWS

## INTRODUCTION

These are arrows of wickedness fired by satanic agents who operate in the occult. Sometimes an image of the victim is used as a point of contact for this wickedness. A lot of the victims complain about receiving bullets in the dream or experiencing discomfort after some sharp objects have entered their bodies. Occult arrows generally emanate oh from wicked meetings where evil decisions are taken against people.

## PRAISE WORSHIP

## PRAYER WARFARE

1. Bring quality repentance unto the Lord.
2. I fire back, every arrow fired at me from the occult world, in the name of Jesus.
3. Let every mirror of darkness and crystal ball monitoring my destiny be shattered to pieces, in the name of Jesus.
4. By the thunder of Your power, O God, arise and scatter every occult conspiracy targeted at me, in Jesus' name.
5. I destroy every material used to represent me in the occult world, in the name of Jesus.
6. O God, arise and let every coven of the powers of the night working against my life be scattered, in the name of Jesus.

7. By the power of the Holy Ghost, and the power in the blood of Jesus, let every arrow of darkness go back to the sender.

8. I wipe away every record of my name in the demonic realm with the blood of Jesus.

9. Every yoke of the oppressor, be broken by fire, in Jesus' name.

10. Let my name become hot coals of fire that cannot be bewitched by any form of occultism, in the name of Jesus.

11. Any power consulting the sun, the moon and the stars against me. be disgraced, in the name of Jesus.

12. Holy Ghost, arise with Your weapons of war, and destroy every habitation of darkness programmed at my progress, in the name of Jesus.

13. Every incantation and enchantment raised against me, be destroyed, in the name of Jesus.

14. Let every token of darkness assigned against me be destroyed by the fire of God, in the name of Jesus.

15. I shall not die but live, to declare the works of the Lord, in the name of Jesus.

16. Let every power of magic and sorcery, designed against me backfire, in the name of Jesus.

17. Any power summoning my name in the spirit realm, be destroyed, in the name of Jesus.

18. In the name that is above all names, the mighty name of Jesus, I barricade my life from every arrow of affliction.

19. Every evil prophet hired to curse me, fall after the order of Balaam, in the name of Jesus.

20. I break and cast out, every arrow of the queen of heaven fired against my destiny, in the name of Jesus.

21. I release myself from curses, spells, jinxes and hexes issued against me by satanic agents, in the name of Jesus.

# 18

# SATANIC POISON

## INTRODUCTION

The spirits responsible for satanic poison introduce physical and spiritual poisons into people's lives. They are introduced to steal, kill and destroy. There are slow poisons and there are fast ones. Occasionally, we have people complaining of eating in the dream, being injected in the dream and having a feeling of lifelessness.

## PRAISE WORSHIP

## PRAYER WARFARE

1. My body, reject every poisonous arrow, in Jesus' name.
2. Let every spiritual poison that has entered into my system, be neutralized by the blood of Jesus.
3. Holy Ghost fire, purge away every handwriting of wickedness, in the name of Jesus.
4. Fire of God, burn to ashes every power programmed into my life to poison me, in the name of Jesus.
5. I command every evil plantation in my life, come out with all your roots, in the name of Jesus! (Lay your hands on your stomach and keep repeating the emphasized are.
6. Evil strangers in my body, come all the way out of your hiding

places, in the name of Jesus.

7. I disconnect any conscious or unconscious link with demonic caterers, in the name of Jesus.

8. Let all avenues of eating or drinking spiritual poisons be closed, in the name of Jesus.

9. I cough out and vomit any food eaten from the table of the devil, in the name of Jesus. *(Cough it out and vomit it by faith. Prime the expulsion).*

10. Let all negative materials circulating in my blood stream be evacuated, in the name of Jesus.

11. I drink the blood of Jesus. *(Physically swallow by faith. Do this for some time.)*

12. Let all evil spiritual feeders warring against me drink their own blood and eat their own flesh, in the name of Jesus.

13. I command all demonic food utensils fashioned against me to be roasted, in the name of Jesus.

14. Holy Ghost fire, circulate all over my body.

15. I command all physical poisons inside my system to be neutralized, in the name of Jesus.

16. Let all evil assignments fashioned against me through the mouth gate be nullified, in the name of Jesus.

17. Let all spiritual problems attached to any hour of the night be cancelled, in the name of Jesus. *(Pick the period from midnight to 6:00 a.m.)*

18. Bread of heaven, fill me till I want no more.

19. Let all catering equipment of evil caterers attached to me be

destroyed, in the name of Jesus.

20. I command my digestive system to reject every evil command, in the name of Jesus.

21. Let all satanic designs of oppression against me in dreams and visions be frustrated, in the name of Jesus.

22. I remove my name from the register of evil feeder with the blood of Jesus.

23. Let the habitation of evil caterers become desolate, in the name of Jesus.

# 19

## DREAM MANIPULATORS

### INTRODUCTION

These are spirits that manipulate victims into error, deception, confusion and destruction through dreams. Negative powers are portrayed as positive and vice-versa. Unscriptural dreams are promoted by these spirits; and such dreams are used as an inspiration by victims, to their own detriment.

## PRAISE WORSHIP

## PRAYER WARFARE

1. Lord, show me dreams and visions that would advance my cause.
2. Let all satanic designs, of oppression against me in dreams and visions be frustrated, in the name of Jesus.
3. Let all the enemies of my good dreams and visions on my home be rendered impotent, in the name of Jesus.
4. I bind the activities of demonic manipulation in dreams and visions, in the name of Jesus.
5. I stand against any defeat in my dreams, in Jesus' name.
6. I claim freedom from satanic and restless dreams, in Jesus' name.
7. I claim all the good things which God has revealed to me through dreams. I reject all satanic dreams, in Jesus' name.

8. (You are going to be specific here. Place your hand on your chest and talk to God specifically about the dreams which need to be cancelled. Cancel it with all your strength. If it needs fire, command the fire of God to burn it to ashes.)

9. O Lord, perform the necessary surgical operation in my life and change all that had gone wrong in the spiritual world.

10. I claim back all the good things which I have lost as a result of defeat and attacks in my dreams, in the name of Jesus.

11. I arrest every spiritual attacker and paralyse their activities in my life, in the name of Jesus.

12. I retrieve my stolen virtues, goodness and blessings, in Jesus' name.

13. Let all satanic manipulations through dreams be dissolved, in the name of Jesus.

14. Let all arrows, gunshots, wounds, oppression and opposition in dreams return to the senders, in the name of Jesus.

15. I reject every evil spiritual load placed on me through dreams, in the name of Jesus.

16. All spiritual animals (cats, dogs, snakes, crocodiles) activated against me, be chained, and returned to the senders, in the name of Jesus.

17. Holy Ghost, purge my intestines and my blood from satanic foods and injections.

18. I break every evil covenant and initiation through dreams, in the name of Jesus.

19. I disband all the hosts of darkness set against me, in Jesus' name.

19. Let all past satanic defeats in the dream be converted to victory, in the name of Jesus.
20. Let all tests in the dream be converted to testimonies, in Jesus' name.
21. Let all trials in the dream be converted to triumphs, in Jesus' name.
22. Let all failures in the dream be converted to success, in Jesus' name.
23. Let all scars in the dream be converted to stars, in Jesus' name.
24. Let all bondage in the dream be converted to freedom, in Jesus' name.
25. Let all losses in the dream be converted to gains, in Jesus' name.
26. Let all oppositions in the dream be converted to victory, in Jesus' name.
27. Let all weaknesses in the dream be converted to strength, in the name of Jesus.
28. Let all negative things in the dream be converted to positive, in Jesus' name.
29. I release myself from every infirmity introduced into my life through dreams, in the name of Jesus.
30. Let all attempts by the enemy to deceive me through dreams fail woefully, in the name of Jesus.
31. I reject evil spiritual husband, wife, children, marriage, engagement, trading, pursuit, ornament, money, friend, relative., etc. in Jesus' name.
32. Lord Jesus, wash my spiritual eyes, ears and mouth with Your

blood.

33. The God who answereth by fire, answer by fire whenever any spiritual attacker comes against me, in Jesus' name.

34. Lord Jesus, replace all satanic dreams with heavenly visions and divinely-inspired dreams.

35. Confess these Scriptures out loud: Psalm 27:1-2, 1Cor. 10:21, Psalm 91.

35. I cancel and wipe off all evil dreams, in the name of Jesus.

36. Let the blood of Jesus erase all evil dreams, in Jesus' name.

37. Let all evil dreams be replaced with blessings, in Jesus' name.

38. I command all my good dreams to come to pass, in Jesus' name.

39. I release myself from every dream pollution, in Jesus' name.

40. Let every satanic attack on my life, in my dreams be converted to victory, in the name of Jesus.

41. Let all rivers, trees, forests, evil companions, evil pursuers, visions of dead relatives, snakes, spirit husbands, spirit wives and masquerades manipulated against me in the dream be completely destroyed by the power in the blood of the Lord Jesus.

42. Every power and spirit in the likeness of snakes attacking me in my dreams, be buried, in the name of Jesus.

43. Let every demonic influence targeted at destroying my vision, dream and ministry receive total disappointment, in Jesus' name.

44. O Lord, enlarge my coasts beyond my widest dream.

45. I stand against every dream of defeat, in Jesus' name.

46. I send the arrows or any gun shot in the dream, back to the senders, in the name of Jesus.

47. I paralyse all the night caterers and I forbid their food in my dream, in the name of Jesus.

48. Let all the contamination in my life through dreams be cleansed by the blood of Jesus.

49. I cancel all visions, dreams, words and curses contrary to my progress, in the name of Jesus.

50. I bind every demon that pollutes spiritual visions and dreams, in the name of Jesus.

51. Divine revelations, spiritual visions, dreams and information will not become scarce commodities in my life, in Jesus' name

52. Every satanic animal in the dream, fall down and die, in Jesus' name.

53. Let all the enemies of my good dreams and visions concerning my home be rendered impotent, in Jesus' name.

54. My imagination and dreams will not be used against me, in Jesus' name.

55. By the blood of Jesus, I rebuke every attacking and fearful dream, in the name of Jesus.

56. Let the evil vision and dream about my life, evaporate from the camp of the enemy, in the name of Jesus.

57. Every cause of demotion in the dream, in my life, be nullified by the blood of Jesus.

58. Every cause of confused and unprogressive dreams, in my life, be nullified by the blood of Jesus.

59. Every cause of harassment in the dreams by familiar faces, be nullified by the blood of Jesus.

60. My dream will not become a nightmare, in Jesus' name.

61. Any anti-progress material fired into my life through dreams, be nullified, in the name of Jesus.

62. By the blood of Jesus, I nullify every dream of... (pick from the under-listed).
- swimming in the water
- eating strange food
- drinking coke and fanta
- having sex with fair or dark women /men
- running without getting to a stop
- talking alone without response
- getting married with a dirty garment
- having or breast-feeding children
- having bald head or hairs falling off
- sitting on a broken or cracked fence
- falling inside the mud
- eating from a broken plate
- getting married without a wedding suit/dress
- sleeping/playing in an uncompleted building

63. Every witchcraft hand planting evil seeds in my life through dreams, wither and burn to ashes, in the name of Jesus.

64. Every marine witchcraft that has introduced spirit husband/wife or child in my dreams, be roasted by fire, in the name of Jesus.

65. Every agent of marine witchcraft posing as my husband, wife or child in my dreams, be roasted by fire, in Jesus' name.

66. Every agent of marine witchcraft assigned to attack my finances through dreams, fall down and perish, in the name of Jesus.

67. Every power or spirit attacking me, in the likeness of snakes in my

dreams, be buried, in the name of Jesus,

68. I command all ny properties captured by spiritual robbers in the dream, to become too hot to handle and come back to me, in the name of Jesus.

69. I bind every demon polluting spiritual vision and dreams, in the name of Jesus,

70. Wonderful Lord, I reverse any defeat that I have ever suffered in the dream, in the name of Jesus.

71. Any dreams that I have dreamt, that are good and for God, I receive them, and those that are satanic, I reject them, in the name of Jesus.

72. Every night and dream attack and its consequences, be nullified, in the name of Jesus.

73. I claim freedom from satanic and restless dreams, in Jesus' name.

74. I claim freedom from importing anxiety and shameful thoughts into my dream, in the name of Jesus.

75. I stand against dream defeats and their effects, in Jesus' name.

76. Let all satanic designs of oppression against me in dreams and visions be frustrated, in the name of Jesus.

77. Let the evil vision and dream on my life evaporate and condense in the camp of the enemy, in the name of Jesus.

78. Every dream of demotion to junior school, be dismantled. I shall go from glory to glory, in the name of Jesus.

79. By the power in the blood of Jesus, I cancel the maturity date of any evil dream concerning my life.

80. O God of promotion, promote me beyond my widest dreams, in the name of Jesus.

81. Every sickness planted into my life through the dream, get out now and go back to your sender, in the name of Jesus.

82. Let life be squeezed out of my dream attackers, in Jesus' name.

83. By the power in the blood of Jesus, I command all my buried good dreams and visions to be exhumed.

84. By the power in the blood of Jesus, I command all my polluted good dreams and visions to receive divine solution.

85. By the power in the blood of Jesus, I command all dream and vision killers, working against the manifestation of my good dreams and visions, to be paralysed.

86. By the power in the blood of Jesus, I command every good dream and vision that have been stolen, to be restored with fresh fire.

87. By the power in the blood of Jesus, I command every good dream and vision that have been transferred, to be restored with fresh fire.

88. By the power in the blood of Jesus, I command every good dream and vision that have been poisoned, to be neutralised,

89. By the power in the blood of Jesus, I command every good dream and vision that have been amputated, to receive divine strength.

90. Let all the contamination in my life through dreams, be cleansed by the blood of Jesus.

91. Any anti-progress material fired into my life through dreams, be nullified, in the name of Jesus.

92. I resist the threat of death in my dream by fire, in Jesus' name.
93. Every evil dream that other people have had about me, I cancel them in the astral world, in the name of Jesus.
94. Every image of Satan in my dream, I curse you to wither now, in the name of Jesus.
95. I command every dream of demotion to stop, in Jesus' name.
96. Every arrow of death in the dream, come out and go back to your sender, in the name of Jesus.
97. Every dream of poverty sponsored by household wickedness against my life, vanish, in the name of Jesus.
98. I dash every poverty dream to the ground, in Jesus' name.
99. I cancel the manipulation of every satanic dream, in Jesus' name.
100. You powers of the night polluting my night dreams, be paralysed, in the name of Jesus.
101. Every anti-prosperity dream, die, in the name of Jesus.
102. Let all satanic designs of oppression against me in dreams and visions be frustrated, in Jesus' name.
103. I paralyse the spirits that bring bad dreams to me, in Jesus' name.
104, I cancel and wipe off all evil dreams, in the name of Jesus.
105. Let the blood of Jesus erase all evil dreams in my life, in Jesus' name.
106. My dreams, my joys, my breakthroughs, that have been buried in the dark world, be resurrected now, in Jesus' name.
107. Every dream serpent, go back to your sender, in Jesus' name.
108. Every power planting affliction into my life in the dream, be

buried alive, in the name of Jesus.

109. Any evil thing that entered into my life through my dream, be dismantled now, in the name of Jesus.

110. O Lord, deliver me from witchcraft dreams.

111. Satanic dreams, go back to your senders, in Jesus' name.

111. I reject satanic dreams, I claim divine revelations, in Jesus' name.

112. You powers of the night polluting my night dreams, be paralysed, in the name of Jesus.

113. Every dream of poverty sponsored by household wickedness against my life, vanish, in the name of Jesus.

114. I drink the blood of Jesus to neutralize every satanic food or drink, taken in the dream, in the name of Jesus.

115. I cancel every evil dream by the blood of Jesus and the fire of the Holy Ghost, in the name of Jesus.

116. Every instrument of satanic retaliation, die, in Jesus' name.

# 20

## SATANIC PROGRAMMERS

### INTRODUCTION

These are spirits that programme evil into people. They give definite instructions on how to do evil successfully. They are in charge of evil inspirations. Their victims waste their lives on unprofitable agenda, even when attempts are made to dissuade them.

### PRAISE WORSHIP

### PRAYER WARFARE

1. Every arrangement of sorcerers and magicians against my destiny, scatter, in the name of Jesus.
2. I withdraw my life from every evil command, in Jesus' name.
3. Let the programme of darkness fashioned against my breakthroughs, be rendered null and void, in Jesus' name.
4. Let my life be too hot for any satanic programmer to handle, in the name of Jesus.
5. I disband every incantation of confusion uttered against me, in Jesus' name.
6. My Father, move by the thunder of your power and disgrace every satanic programmer, in the name of Jesus.
7. Lord, release Your angels of war to destroy every programme of

the enemy for my destiny, in Jesus' name.

8. Every altar of affliction, be dismantled by fire, in Jesus' name.

9. Spirit of the living God, overshadow my life and barricade it from every dart of the enemy, in the name of Jesus.

10. O God arise, and let every satanic programme for my destiny scatter, in the name of Jesus.

11. Every power dragging me to the tail, I disconnect you, in the name of Jesus.

12. O God of Abraham Isaac and Jacob, raise helpers for me in hidden places, in the name of Jesus.

13. I shall be an unconquerable warrior, in the name of Jesus.

14. O eagle of my life, reject every programme of demotion, in the name of Jesus.

15. Holy Ghost fire, burn to ashes every programme of darkness in my dream, in the name of Jesus.

16. I shall mount up with wings as the eagle, in Jesus' name.

17. I break every spell, curse or enchantment programmed against me, in the name of Jesus.

18. By the power that divided the Red Sea, let the programme of any strongman designed for me turn against him, in the name of Jesus.

19. Thou power of the oppressor, come out of my life and enter no more, in the name of Jesus.

20. Every power that kills opportunities, I bury you alive, in the name of Jesus.

21. I slay the giant in the garden of my destiny, in Jesus' name.

22. I receive angelic assistance to overcome the power of the shadow of death, in the name of Jesus.

23. Blood of Jesus, arise with Your weapon of war and put to shame every arrangement of darkness, in the name of Jesus.

24. I arise and go forth to conquer, in the name of Jesus.

25. Every satanic programme, I render you impotent, in Jesus' name.

26. Handwriting of the blood of Jesus, write victory on my forehead, in the name of Jesus.

# 11

# WICKED TERMINATORS

## INTRODUCTION

These are spirits that cause tragic termination of good things. They programme tragedies and disasters that result in wastage of life and property. They sweep off promising lives and plans in one full swing of tragedy.

## PRAISE WORSHIP

## PRAYER WARFARE

1. I terminate the activity of the terminator, in Jesus' name.
2. O yoke of the power of death, break, in Jesus' name.
3. I shall not die but live to declare the works of God, in Jesus' name.
4. I bind and put to shame every eater of flesh and drinker of blood, in the name of Jesus.
5. Every power that does not want to see me alive, loose your hold, in the name of Jesus.
6. I shall not absorb any evil arrow that flies by day or by night, in the name of Jesus.
7. Let Your power, O Lord, fill my life to the brim, in Jesus' name.

8. Every ordination of the terminator, I command you to fail, in the name of Jesus,
9. By the power that cut off the head of Goliath, let the head of terminators, be cut off, in the name of Jesus.
10. By the anointing which breaks every yoke, every power masquerading to do me harm, I bury you today, in Jesus' name.
11. I plead the blood of Jesus over every pronouncement of death fashioned against me, in the name of Jesus.
12. O glory of God, arise and shine in my life, in Jesus' name.
13. Let the rain of blessings fall upon me and quench every terminating fire, in the name of Jesus.
14. You wicked terminators, I bind you and cast you out, in the name of Jesus.
15. Every weapon of oppression, be destroyed by the fire of the God of Elijah, in the name of Jesus.
16. Every power that walks about at night, to wage war against me, I bury you alive, in the name of Jesus.
17. Spirit of the God of Elijah, arise in Your fire, terminate the terminators, in the name of Jesus.
18. Holy Ghost fire, baptise me in a fresh way, in Jesus' name.
19. Every satanic pronouncement uttered against my destiny, be dismantled, in the name of Jesus.
20. I shall not come to this world in vain, in the name of Jesus.
21. I receive power to defeat defeat, in the name of Jesus.
22. I receive power to put every enemy of my destiny to flight, in the name of Jesus.
23. Let Your arm of love, O Lord, encircle me always, in Jesus' name.

# 22
# BACKSLIDING SPIRIT

## INTRODUCTION

These are spirits that sponsor lukewarmness, carelessness, secret sins, cleverly-concealed atrocities, slumber and other iniquities. They drain out spiritual energy and quench the 'first love' (Rev. 3).

### PRAISE WORSHIP

### PRAYER WARFARE

1. Bring quality repentance unto the Lord.
2. Holy Ghost fire, pour liquid fire into my soul, in Jesus' name.
3. Every rough place in my spiritual life, be made plain by the blood of Jesus.
4. I shall mount up with wings as eagles, in Jesus' name.
5. I shall be a warrior in the army of the Lord, in Jesus' name.
6. I bind and cast out every spirit of lukewarmness, in the name of Jesus.
7. Holy Ghost fire, fall on me to energise my life, in Jesus' name.
8. I shall not lack oil on my spiritual head, in Jesus' name.

9. Let fresh fire from heaven fall on me now, in Jesus' name
10 I receive the anointing to break every yoke of the oppressor, in the name of Jesus.
11 Let every power of procrastination melt away from my spiritual man, in the name of Jesus.
12. I shall arise and destroy every shackle of spiritual slavery, in the name of Jesus.
13. Let the yoke of backsliding be broken, in Jesus' name.
14. I shall not turn back from following the Lord, in Jesus' name.
15. I shall not bow down to any evil image placed before me, in the name of Jesus.
16. I receive strength to overcome the arrows of the tempter, in the name of Jesus.
17. Let the fire of God destroy every plantation of darkness working against my life, in the name of Jesus.
18. My Glory and the Lifter of my head, lift me up by fire, in the name of Jesus.
19. Blood of Jesus, wash me and make me whole, in Jesus' name.
20. Holy Ghost fire, purge my life, in the name of Jesus.
21. I release myself from any inherited bondage and limitations, in the name of Jesus.
22, O Lord, send Your axe of fire to the foundation of my life and destroy every evil plantation.
23. Let the blood of Jesus flush out from my system every inherited satanic deposit, in the name of Jesus.
24. I release myself from the grip of any problem transferred into my life from the womb, in the name of Jesus.

25. Let the blood of Jesus and the fire of the Holy Ghost cleanse every organ in my body, in the name of Jesus.
26. I break and loose myself from every inherited evil covenant, in the name of Jesus.
27. I break and loose myself from every inherited evil curse, in the name of Jesus.
28. I vomit every evil thing that I have been fed with as a child in the name of Jesus.
29. I command all foundational strongmen attached to my life to be paralysed, in the name of Jesus.
30. Let any rod of the wicked rising against my family line be rendered impotent for my sake, in the name of Jesus.
31. I cancel the consequences of any evil local name attached to my person, in the name of Jesus.
32. Pray aggressively against the following evil foundations. Pray as follows: You (pick the under-listed one by one), loose your hold over my life and be purged out of my foundation, in Jesus' name.

- destructive effect of polygamy
- evil physical design
- unscriptural manner of conception
- parental curses
- envious rivalry
- demonic blood transfusion
- evil dedication
- demonic alteration of destiny
- demonic incisions
- demonic marriage
- dream pollution
- evil laying on of hands
- demonic sacrifice
- fellowship with family idols
- fellowship with local idols

- fellowship with demonic consultants
- wrong exposure to sex - exposure to evil diviner
- demonic initiations - inherited infirmity

33. You evil foundational plantations, come out of my life with all your roots in the name of Jesus.
34. I break and loose myself from every form of demonic bewitchment in the name of Jesus.
35. I release myself from every evil domination and control in the name of Jesus.
36. Let the blood of Jesus be transfused into my blood vessel.
37. Let every gate opened to the enemy by my foundation be closed forever with the blood of Jesus.
38. Lord Jesus, walk back into every second of my life and deliver me where I need deliverance, heal me where I need healing. transform me where I need transformation.
39. Let the power in the blood of Jesus separate me from the sins of my ancestors.
40. Let the blood of Jesus remove any unprogressive label from every aspect of my life.
41. O Lord, create in me a clean heart by Your power.
42. O Lord, renew a right spirit within me.
43. O Lord, teach me to die to self.
44, O Lord, ignite my calling with Your fire.
45. O Lord, anoint me to pray without ceasing.
46. O Lord, establish me as a holy person unto You.

47. O Lord, restore my spiritual eyes and ears.
48. O Lord, let the anointing to excel in my spiritual and physical life fall on me.
49. O Lord, produce in me the power of self-control and gentleness
50. O Lord, let the anointing of the Holy Spirit break every yoke of backwardness in my life.
51. Holy Ghost, breathe on me now, in the name of Jesus.
52. Holy Ghost fire, ignite me to the glory of God.
53. Let every rebellion flee from my heart, in Jesus' name.
54. I command every spiritual contamination in my life to receive cleansing by the blood of Jesus.
55. Let the brush of the Lord scrub out every dirtiness in my spiritual pipe, in the name of Jesus.
56. Every rusted spiritual pipe in my life, receive wholeness, in the name of Jesus.
57. I command every power eating up my spiritual pipe to be roasted, in the name of Jesus.
58. I renounce any evil dedication placed upon my life, in Jesus' name.
59. I break every evil edict and ordination, in Jesus' name.
60. O Lord, cleanse all the soiled part of my life.
61. O Lord, deliver me from every foundational Pharaoh.
62. O Lord, heal every wounded part of my life.
63. O Lord, bend every evil rigidity in my life.
64. O Lord, re-align every stray of satanic nature in my life.
65. O Lord, let the fire of the Holy Spirit warm every satanic frost

in my life.

66. O Lord, give me a life that kills death.
67. O Lord, kindle in me the fire of charity.
68. O Lord, glue me together where I am opposed to myself.
69. O Lord, enrich me with Your gifts.
70. O Lord, quicken me and increase my desire for the things of heaven.
71. By Your rulership, O Lord, let the lust of the flesh in my life die.
72. Lord Jesus, increase daily in my life.
73. Lord Jesus, maintain your gifts in my life.
74. O Lord, refine and purge my life by Your fire.
75. Holy Spirit, set my heart on fire, in the name of Jesus.
76. Holy Ghost fire, begin to burn away every power of the bond woman in me, in the name of Jesus.
77. O Lord, make me ready to go wherever You send me.
78. Lord Jesus, never let me shut You out.
79. Lord Jesus, work freely in me and through me.

## INTRODUCTION

These are major evil warring spirits of the last days. They lead men and women into sexual perversion, strange doctrines, immorality, evil distraction and lust. They are spirits that sponsor evil diversions.

These are spirits that deceive and mislead. They invite corruption and spiritual blindness. They open the gate for heresies, false bickering and silent destruction.

# 23
# SEDUCTIVE SPIRITS

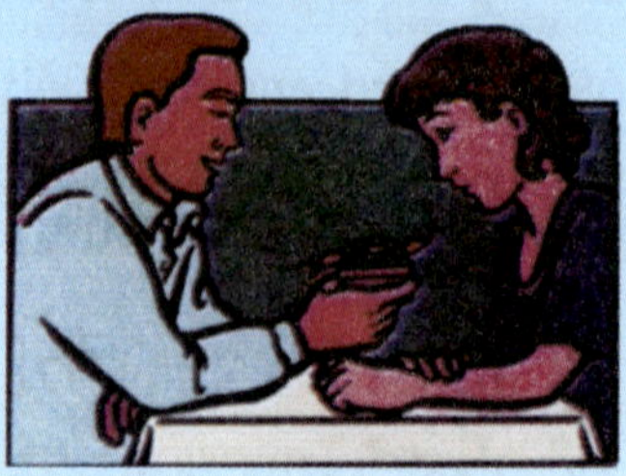

### PRAISE WORSHIP

### PRAYER WARFARE

1. Bring quality repentance unto the Lord.
2. I bind and cast out every spirit of sexual perversion, in the name of Jesus.
3. Every arrow of the tempter, backfire, in Jesus' name.
4. Let the fire of God burn to ashes every plantation of whoredom in my life, in the name of Jesus.
5. I receive deliverance from every power of the oppressor, in the name of Jesus.
6. Thou power of seduction, die, in the name of Jesus.

7 I shall not die but live to declare the works of God, in Jesus' name.

8 I shall not be caged by the power of seduction, in Jesus' name.

9. Every strange flesh harassing my destiny, die, in Jesus' name

10. Any power pulling me to iniquity, be destroyed, in Jesus' name.

11. Every plantation of seduction in my body, be wiped away, in the name of Jesus.

12. Holy Ghost fire, move me away from the powers and activities of the flesh, in the name of Jesus.

13. My life, reject every evil attraction, in the name of Jesus.

14. I bind and cast out every demon in my reproductive organ, in the name of Jesus.

15. I shall not mortgage my calling on the altar of sex, in Jesus' name.

16. I shall rise above any sexual hook, in Jesus' name.

17. My inner man, reject the hook of seduction, in Jesus' name.

18. Every yoke of the oppressor, break, in Jesus' name.

19. I withdraw any organ of my body from every evil altar, in the name of Jesus.

20. I release myself from the grip of any strange man / woman, in the name of Jesus.

21. Let the yoke of seduction be broken, in Jesus' name.

22, Every spirit of Delilah that is pursuing my calling. be buried alive, in the name of Jesus.

23. Every Jezebe!l power, loose your hold, in Jesus' name.

# 24

# ROCK DEMONS

## INTRODUCTION

These are wicked, stubborn and terrible demons common in mountainous or rocky areas. They originate tragedy idolatry, resistance to the gospel, environmental poverty and general hard life for the victims.

## PRAISE WORSHIP

**Confess these words with faith in your heart three times.**

Oh Lord, my God, I thank you for loving me. I know you have good things in stock for me. Lord Jesus, I thank you for Your steadfast love and faithfulness to me and my family. My Father and my God, as I open my mouth to pray these warfare prayer points, Oh Lord, answer me by fire, in the name of Jesus.

## PRAYER WARFARE

1. I receive power to overcome every spirit of the rock, in the name of Jesus.
2. You spirit of the rock, release my destiny by fire, in Jesus' name.
3. You power of the rock, release my blessings by the blood of Jesus
4. All my blessings deposited inside the rock, receive fire and locate me now, in the name of Jesus.

5. You power of the rock, assigned to afflict me, die, in Jesus' name.
6 Every rock of poverty, break and release my money by fire, in the name of Jesus.
7 Anything inside the rock programmed against me, break to pieces, in the name of Jesus.
8. Rock of Ages, fight against every rock of failure in my life, in the name of Jesus.
9. Every evil load in my life, come out by fire, in Jesus' name.
10. Anything planted in my life by the enemy, die, in Jesus' name.
11. You evil stone in my body, come out by fire, in Jesus' name.
12. Every stone of problem in my life, die, in Jesus' name.
13. Oh Lord, purge me with your fire, in the name of Jesus.
14. Every evil material in my body, die, by fire, in Jesus' name.
15. Every evil monitoring power inside the rock assigned against my life, break by fire, in the name of Jesus.
16. Thank the Lord for answered prayers.

# 25

# FOREST DEMONS

## INTRODUCTION

These are forest spirits that demand worship. In many places, they bring terror to the natives and sponsor tragedies and environmental disasters when not worshipped. Many farmers consciously or unconsciously pay homage to them.

## PRAISE WORSHIP

## PRAYER WARFARE

1. I speak unto the wind to carry destructive warfare into the camp of forest spirits, in the name of Jesus.
2. Every yoke of forest spirits, be broken, in Jesus' name.
3. I arrest every operation and activity of forest spirits, in the name of Jesus.
4. Every manipulation targeted against my destiny from the forest, be disgraced, in the name of Jesus.
5. I blow off every forest altar, in the name of Jesus.
6. Let the east wind blow away every plan of forest sorcerers, in the name of Jesus.
7 O Lord, let Your military angels pass through every forest waging warfare against me, in the name of Jesus.

8 Let the earthquake of fire destroy the handwriting of darkness fashioned against me by forest demons, in Jesus' name.

9. Every plan of forest sorcerers working against my breakthroughs, be disgraced, in Jesus' name

10. I reverse every forest incantation fashioned against my destiny, in the name of Jesus.

11. Holy Ghost fire, arise with Your weapons of war and demolish every stronghold of darkness in the forest, in the name of Jesus.

12. I shall not be subjected to any manipulation from forest spirits, in the name of Jesus.

13. Every evil tree working against my breakthroughs, be uprooted by fire, in the name of Jesus.

14. Let my destiny reject every handwriting of forest demons, in the name of Jesus.

15. Holy Ghost fire, burn to ashes every plan of forest sorcerers, working against my life, in the name of Jesus.

16. Every satanic summon of my spirit-man from the forest, be disgraced, in the name of Jesus.

17. Let every forest animal targeted at my life be disgraced, in the name of Jesus.

18. I arrest every spirit of the grave working against my life, in the name of Jesus.

19. Every power in the forest targeting my destiny for destruction, be disgraced, in the name of Jesus.

20. I pull down every stronghold of darkness in the forest fashioned against my destiny, in the name of Jesus.

21. Let every spirit ministering against me in any satanic altar be de- robed and disgraced, in the name of Jesus.
22. Every star hunter targeting my life for destruction, be disgraced, in the name of Jesus.
23. Let the spirit of Elijah wage war against all satanic prophets ministering at forest altars, in the name of Jesus.
24. O God, arise and let all forest strongholds be scattered, in the name of Jesus.
25. Every power chanting my name on forest altars, be disgraced, in the name of Jesus.
26. Holy Ghost fire, move upon my life in a new way, in Jesus' name.
27. I refuse to be enslaved by any forest power, in Jesus' name.

## INTRODUCTION

This is one of the strongmen identified in the book of Revelation. This spirit sponsors death, killer diseases, incurable diseases, terminal sicknesses and other horrible causes of death

# 26

# SPIRIT OF DEATH AND HELL

### PRAISE WORSHIP

### PRAYER WARFARE

1. Thank God for the power of resurrection and life.
2. I release myself from every curse of untimely death, in the name of Jesus.
3. I break every unprofitable covenant of untimely death, in the name of Jesus.
4. I remove my life from every shadow of death, in Jesus' name
5. I bind and paralyse every strongman of death and hell, in the name of Jesus.
6. Lord, strengthen my body, soul and spirit.
7. Let every secret about battles against my spiritual life be revealed, in the name of Jesus.
8. I reject and release myself from the grip of the spirit of infirmity, in the name of Jesus.
9. I drink the blood of Jesus into the whole of my system.

10, Lord, build around me the hedge of fire.

11. Let the spirit of life replace the spirit of death in my life, in the name of Jesus.

12. Woe unto the demonic vessel that the enemy would use to cause me spiritual injury. in the name of Jesus.

13. Father Lord, let Your glory cover every aspect of my life, in Jesus' name.

14. Father Lord, let Your angels encamp around me, in Jesus' name.

15. I renounce and break every death covenant that I have made or which anyone has made on my behalf, in Jesus' name.

16. I remove the control of my life from the hands of any dead person, in the name of Jesus.

17. I stand against every covenant of sudden death, in Jesus' name.

18, Every blessing of mine that has been buried in the ground or under any water, be released by fire, in Jesus' name.

19. I cancel my name from every death register, in Jesus' name

20. I stand against every form of tragedy, in Jesus' name.

21. Every grave cloth over my life, be removed by fire, in Jesus' name.

22. All my potentials that have been destroyed, receive life now, in the name of Jesus.

23. I stand against all the powers that push a person to hell fire, in the name of Jesus.

# 27

# AFFLICTION REVIVERS

## INTRODUCTION

**Nahum 1:9:** What do ye imagine against the Lord? he will make an utter end: affliction shall not rise up the second time.

These are spirits that open old wounds and ignite the resurrection of afflictions. They manipulate people to go back into old sins which would then bring back old afflictions.

## PRAISE WORSHIP

## PRAYER WARFARE

1. Any power reviving bad things in my life, be disgraced, in the name of Jesus.
2. Affliction will not rise again in my life, in the name of Jesus.
3. Every handwriting of affliction, I wipe you off by the power in the blood of Jesus.
4. Every power targeted at my peace, be disgraced, in Jesus' name
5. Every altar of affliction prepared for my destiny, I pull you down, in the name of Jesus.
6. Every power working against my good health, I command you to be disgraced, in the name of Jesus.

7. I bind and cast out every oppressive spirit, in Jesus' name.
8. I shall not be a victim of repeated oppression, in Jesus' name
9. My destiny, reject every circle of affliction, in Jesus' name.
10. Spirit of the living God, arise in Your power and put to shame any power that wants to put me to shame, in Jesus' name.
11, Holy Ghost fire, burn to ashes every plantation of affliction, in the name of Jesus.
12. Every yoke of the oppressor, be broken, in Jesus' name.
13. My body, reject every handwriting of infirmity, in Jesus' name.
14. My life, reject every handwriting of affliction, in Jesus' name.
15. I arise by the Spirit of God to torment every tormentor and oppress every oppressor, in the name of Jesus.
16. Every power that does not want to see me around, be buried alive, in the name of Jesus.
17. Let the disgrace of my enemies be multiplied, in Jesus' name.
18. Let all my problems become my promotion, in Jesus' name.
19. Fire of God, move by thunder of Your power and pursue every affliction out of my life, in the name of Jesus.
20. I shall arise by the power of God and disgrace any power that wants to disgrace me, in the name of Jesus.
21. By the Spirit of the living God, I overcome every satanic handwriting targeted at my peace, in Jesus' name.
22. O God arise, and usher me into continuous victory, in Jesus' name.
23. The name of the Lord, which is a strong tower, move upon my life today, and let every handwriting of affliction die, in Jesus' name.

24. O power of God, appear in every situation that wants to put me to shame, and oppress my oppressor, in Jesus' name.

25. My Glory and the Lifter of my head, move upon my situation and make me an overcomer, in the name of Jesus.

26. I arise above all arrows of afflictions, by the power in the blood of Jesus.

27. Every yoke of the oppressor, be dashed to pieces, in Jesus' name.

28. Any power using my name for bewitchment, I pull you down, in the name of Jesus.

29. By the thunder of Your power, O God arise, and disgrace my oppressors, in the name of Jesus.

30. I bind and cast out any power introducing affliction into my life, in the name of Jesus.

# 28
# SPIRITS OF DIVIṈATON

## INTRODUCTION
**Acts 16:16-18**

These are spirits responsible for fortune telling, witchcraft, necromancy horoscope, astrology and hypnotism, the practices of which are forbidden in the Scriptures (Deut. 18:9-12).

**PRAISE WORSHIP**

**PRAYER WARFARE**

1. Every power divining against my destiny, die, in Jesus' name.
2. Every divination targeted at my moving forward, perish, in the name of Jesus.
3. Every power chanting incantations against me, be disgraced, in the name of Jesus.
4. Holy Ghost fire, burn to ashes every crystal ball observing my life, in the name of Jesus.
5. No enchantment or divination fashioned against my destiny shall prosper, in the name of Jesus.
6. I refuse to be a victim of divination, in Jesus' name.
7. Every yoke of divination working against my life, be broken, in the

name of Jesus.

8. Every satanic priest divining against my star, be disgraced, in the name of Jesus.

9. Thou divining powers targeted at my progress, die, in Jesus' name.

10. Every power assigned to summon my spirit, I pull you down, in the name of Jesus,

11. Every divining priest hired against my life, I render you mad, in the name of Jesus.

12. I render my life immune from every operation of divination, in the name of Jesus.

13. I shall be an overcomer over every negative divining power, in the name of Jesus.

14. I shall not surrender to any power of divination, in Jesus name.

15. My life, refuse to take instructions from any divination in the heavenlies, in the name of Jesus.

16. By the power of the Holy Ghost, I rise above every divination, in the name of Jesus.

17. Spirit of the living God, speak to me by Your power and nullify every word uttered against me by divining powers, in Jesus' name.

18. I reverse every word uttered against me by divining powers, in the name of Jesus.

19. Every conspiracy in the heavenlies fashioned against my breakthroughs, I command it to be disgraced, in Jesus' name.

20. Spirit of the living God, anoint me for total breakthroughs against every oppressive power, in the name of Jesus.

21. Let my life pick up fire that cannot be overcome by any power of

enchantment, in the name of Jesus.

22. O God, arise and let every plan of diviners for my life be scattered, in the name of Jesus.
23. I arise above every enchantment of the diviners, in Jesus' name.
24. Spirit of the living God, overshadow my life by Your power, in the name of Jesus.
25. Thou divining power of my father's house, hear the word of the living God, evaporate, in the name of Jesus.
26. Thou divining power of my mother's house, hear the word of the living God, evaporate, in the name of Jesus.
27. By the anointing that breaks the yoke, let every yoke of divination be broken, in the name of Jesus.
28. Every power harassing my destiny with incantations, be disgraced, in the name of Jesus.

# 29

# DEVOURING SPIRIT

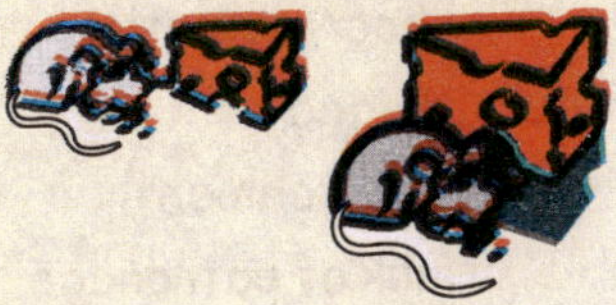

## INTRODUCTION

**Malachi 3:8-12**

The operations of devouring spirits manifest as abject poverty, inability to remain financially afloat and perpetual indebtedness, Anyone under the control of this spirit would always suffer from financial failure, bad timing, constant duping, inability to save money and leaking pockets. A regular trend of destruction of properties also follow.

## PRAISE WORSHIP

## PRAYER WARFARE

1. I bind and cast out every devouring spirit, in Jesus' name.
2. Let the yoke of the devourers be broken to pieces, in Jesus' name.
3. I shall arise above every destructive power, in Jesus' name.
4. Let the cankerworm and the caterpillar assigned against my breakthroughs be disgraced, in the name of Jesus.
5. Thou power of foundational poverty, die, in Jesus' name.
6. O God, arise and let every enemy of my prosperity scatter, in the name of Jesus.
7. Spirit of the living God, arise in Your power and arrest every financial arrester, in the name of Jesus.
8. Any power making me to eat my tithes and offerings, loose your hold, in the name of Jesus.

9. Father, in the name of Jesus, advertise Your prosperity in my life
10. I bind and cast out from my life, every spirit of.. . (pick from the under-listed), in the name of Jesus.
    - failure at the edge of breakthroughs
    - financial destruction
    - lack of foresight
    - procrastination
    - tragedy
    - bewitchment
    - lack of patronage
    - manipulation of helpers
    - property destruction
    - closed heaven
    - destructive incantations
    - poor management
    - stinginess to God
    - laziness
    - backwardness
    - unexplainable losses
    - business failure
    - dream manipulation
    - marital destruction
    - robbery
11. Let every satanic vulture despatched against my progress be arrested, in the name of Jesus.
12. Every money-devouring infirmity, loose your hold, in Jesus' name.
13. I release myself from every yoke of the devourer, in Jesus' name.
14. I pull down the stronghold of the devouring spirit, in Jesus' name.
15. I cancel and reverse every curse of poverty, in Jesus' name.
16. Let my life experience a turn-around breakthrough, in Jesus name.

# 30
# SPIRITUAL GUNMEN

INTRODUCTION

These are spiritual powers that specialise in spiritual assassinations. They appear in the spirit as gunmen shooting to kill. Many victims who have experienced their battles, never woken up the next morning. Satanic agents hire such powers to eliminate their opponents.

## PRAISE WORSHIP

## PRAYER WARFARE

1. I fire back every satanic bullet targeted at my breakthroughs, in the name of Jesus.
2. I fire back every spiritual bullet targeted at my dream life, in the name of Jesus.
3. Let spiritual gunmen, gun themself down, in Jesus' name.
4. Thou bullet of darkness, locate your gunman, in Jesus' name.
5. I shall not be a victim of satanic bullet, in the name of Jesus.
6. Every power aimed at shooting down my spirit-man, shoot down

yourself, in the name of Jesus.

7. I take divine insurance against every physical or spiritual hired assassin, in the name of Jesus.
8. O God arise, and let spiritual gunmen scatter, in Jesus' name.
9. By the thunder of Your power, O Lord, speak confusion into the camp of spiritual killers, in the name of Jesus.
10. My Father, speak confusion into the camp of my organised enemies, in the name of Jesus.
11. I shall not die but live to praise the Lord, in Jesus' name.
12. Blood of Jesus, arise in Your power, envelope my life and fight for me, in the name of Jesus.
13. Every power hired to assassinate my spirit-man, fall after the order of Balaam, in the name of Jesus.
14. Let the imagination of the spiritual gunman hired against me fail, in the name of Jesus.
15. Every handwriting of the oppressor, be wiped out, in the name of Jesus.
16. Every evil eye monitoring my life for attack, die, in Jesus' name.
17. By the power of the Holy Ghost, I fire back every witchcraft arrow, in the name of Jesus.
18. Fire of God, burn to ashes every handwriting of oppressors, in the name of Jesus.
19. I bind and cast out every ladder of darkness, in Jesus' name.
20. O God, arise and let all wicked powers monitoring my life scatter, in the name of Jesus.
21. You terror of the night, scatter, in the name of Jesus.

22. O God, put to shame every enemy of my well-being, in Jesus' name.
23. Every satanic soldier appearing in my dream, be buried alive, in the name of Jesus.
24. Power of God, pursue every spiritual gunman pursuing my life, in the name of Jesus.
25. Every satanic instruction given to any power to eliminate me, backfire, in the name of Jesus.
26. Every evil magnet of spiritual attacks, die, in Jesus' name.
27. I shake myself loose from every terror of the night and every arrow that flies by the day, in the name of Jesus.

# 31

# BREAKTHROUGH AMPUTATORS

## INTRODUCTION

These are spirits that initiate the near-success syndrome or failure at the edge of breakthroughs.

PRAISE WORSHIP

## PRAYER WARFARE

1. I confess my sins of exhibiting occasional doubts.
2. Let the angels of the living God roll away the stone blocking my financial, physical and spiritual breakthroughs, in Jesus' name.
3. I bind every spirit manipulating my beneficiaries against me the name of Jesus.
4. I remove my name from the book of dreamers of goodness without realisation, in the name of Jesus.
5. O God, arise and let all the enemies of my breakthroughs scatter, in the name of Jesus.
6. Let the fire of God melt away the stones hindering my blessings, in the mighty name of Jesus.
7. Let the cloud blocking the sunlight of my glory and breakthrough be dispersed, in Jesus' name.
8. All secrets of the enemy in the camp of my life, that are still in

darkness, be revealed to me now, in Jesus' name.

9. All evil spirits masquerading as friends in order to trouble me, be bound, in the name of Jesus.
10. Lord, let me not put unprofitable and heavy loads upon myself, in the name of Jesus.
11. All keys to my goodness that are still in the possession of the enemy, Lord, give them unto me.
12. Open my eyes, O Lord, and let my ways be not darkened before me.
13. All my sweat on the affairs of my life will not be in vain, in the name of Jesus.
14. The pregnancy of good things within me will not be aborted by any evil power, in the name of Jesus.
15. Lord, turn me to untouchable coal of fire.
16. Lord, let wonderful changes begin to be my lot from this week.
17. Lord, remove covetousness from my eyes.
18. Lord, fill the cup of my life to the brim.
19. Let every power stepping on my goodness receive the arrow of fire of God now, in the name of Jesus.
20. I reject every spirit of the tail in all areas of my life, in the name of Jesus.
21. Thank God for the victory.

# 32

# TRAGEDY ACTIVATORS

INTRODUCTION

They are spirits that initiate and activate sorrowful events and tragedies. For example, a driver knows that he should not drink before driving, but these spirits will encourage him to drink. They are wicked powers that prepare errors which result in tragic loss of lives.

## PRAISE WORSHIP

## PRAYER WARFARE

1. Every power activating tragedy in my life, die, in Jesus' name.
2 The sun shall not smite me by day, nor the moon by night, in the name of Jesus.
3. Every weapon fashioned against my safety, be destroyed, in the name of Jesus.
4. I take divine insurance against every form of accident and tragedy, in the name of Jesus.
5. Let the protective power of God cover my life, in Jesus' name.
6. Blood of Jesus, destroy every plan of the enemy against my well-being, in the name of Jesus.
7. By Your unfailing power, O Lord, let me become untouchable coals of fire, in the name of Jesus.
8. Every imagination of the enemy against my breakthroughs, be

dismantled, in the name of Jesus.

9. Holy Ghost fire, scatter and shatter to pieces every plan of the enemy for my life, in the name of Jesus,
10. Anything programmed into the heavenlies against my safety, be dismantled, in the name of Jesus.
11. I cover myself and all my journeys with the blood of Jesus.
12. Power of the oppressor, my life is not your victim, in Jesus' name.
13. All environmental planners of evil, scatter, in Jesus' name
14. My spirit-man, arise by the fire and thunder of God, and disgrace every tragedy activator working against me, in the name of Jesus.
15. I refuse to be a victim for eaters of flesh and drinkers of blood, in the name of Jesus.
16. My blood shall not be available on any altar of Satan, in Jesus' name
17. I shall run and not be weary, and walk and not faint, in Jesus' name.
18. Every power planning tragedy for me, be disgraced, in Jesus' name.
19. Every conspiracy against my well-being, melt away, in Jesus' name.
20. Power of God, move against every witchcraft attack working against me, in the name of Jesus.
21, O God, arise and let all the enemies of my peace, Scatter, in the name of Jesus.
22. By the power of the Holy Ghost, I arise to overcome every environmental serpent and scorpion, in the name of Jesus.
23. O God that sitteth in the heavens, laugh to scorn every power conspiring against my life, in the name of Jesus.

24. Anything in my life that would remove my shield of protection, be destroyed, in the name of Jesus.
25. Blood of Jesus, fire of God, surround and barricade me from every arrow of darkness, in the name of Jesus.
26. Bewitchment shall not capture my vessel of transportation, in the name of Jesus.

## INTRODUCTION

Hidden curses are the most wicked weapons used by the devil, the enemy of our souls. You owe yourself the duty of reversing all hidden curses in your life. Your life will be transformed the moment all hidden curses are cancelled. You will begin to experience the joy of living life at its fullest.

# 33

# CURSE ENFORCING SPTRITS

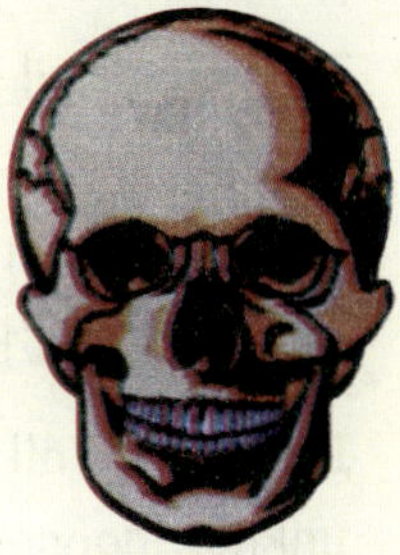

### PRAISE WORSHIP

### PRAYER WARFARE

1. Lord Jesus, I confess to You that I have been in bondage in the following areas (name the specific areas), and I ask You to reveal to me the cause or causes that brought about this. (Here, confess to the Lord whatever He brings to your mind) I thank You for the release that You gained for me when You became a curse on the cross.

2. I ask You to forgive me or my ancestors for any sin that has exposed me to a curse *(name any specific sin that you are aware of,)* I receive Your forgiveness and I choose to forgive those who have sinned against me *(name these people)*

3. I break any ungodly ties that still bind me to anyone in my life, who has ever hurt or disappointed me, or to whom I have related

in an ungodly way. *(Name these people as you break the unhealthy bonds and 'soul ties')*

4. I renounce all contacts with the occult and promise to destroy all occult objects that I possess. *(Name the specific occult involvement.)*
5. I renounce all sexual sins, and I break the power of pornography that may have a hold of me.
6. I renounce all self-inflicted curses that I have pronounced on myself, and I break those patterns from my heart and tongue.
7. I renounce all curses that I have issued, whether knowingly or unknowingly: gossip, bitter words, anger and judgement. I break the authority of any occult power in my life.
8. I renounce all unholy covenants which I or my ancestors have made *(name them)*.
9. I renounce all patterns of stinginess with finances that I or my ancestors possessed. I resolve to be obedient to the Lord in the area of tithes and offerings.
10. I renounce all attitudes of reliance upon man and the flesh. I resolve to put my trust solely in the Lord, my God.
11. I once and for all, release myself from the power and authorities of any curse.
12. All demonic spirits and powers involved *(name them if they are discerned)*, I bind you and command you to cease your activities in my life and to leave my life, my body, my soul, my mind, my family, my house, my job, etc.
13. I say all these prayer points in the authority of the name of Jesus and give You thanks and praise, Lord, that all these things are done.

## 34

# CHILDREN KILLERS

## INTRODUCTION

**Exod. 20:12: Deut. 18:10**

These are terrible spirits with hatred for children. They pursue an agenda of hatred, demonic initiations, bad company, youthful exuberance, and disobedience. This is to shorten the lives of the young ones or eliminate them outrightly. The Bible says, "Honour thy father and thy mother so that thy days may be long." These spirits make the young ones to be rebellious, and dishonour their parents so that their days can be short.

These spirits are also responsible for abortions, sexual abuse of children, violence and anti-social attitudes exhibited by the youth. The spirits of children killers were functional in the days of king Herod. The ultimate agenda of these spirits is to divert or destroy destinies.

## PRAISE WORSHIP

## PRAYER WARFARE

1 Every power of Herod pursuing my children, be destroyed, in the name of Jesus.

2. I refuse to release my children into the hands of destiny

arresters, in the name of Jesus.

In numbers 3 - 20, mention the name

3. I break the hold of every witchcraft initiation upon ..., in the name of Jesus.
4. Every destructive power, release ... in the name of Jesus.
5. Every power that does not want.. . to live long, be disgraced, in the name of Jesus.
6. Holy Ghost fire, release . .. from every evil association, in the name of Jesus.
7. Blood of Jesus, deliver...from the hand of the oppressors, in the name of Jesus.
8. Every agenda of untimely death for..., be dismantled, in the name of Jesus.
9. I fire back every arrow of familiar spirit targeted at..., in the name of Jesus.
10. I fire back every arrow of witchcraft targeted at .. , in the name of Jesus.
11. Power of God, move . . forward, whether the devil likes it or not, in the name of Jesus.
12. Every rage of destiny-killers against . .., be dismantled, in the name of Jesus,
13. I decree that insanity is not the lot of. .., in Jesus' name.
14. I decree that addictions are not the lot of ..., in Jesus' name
15. Every behaviour contrary to God in the life..., melt away, by the blood of Jesus.
16. Holy Ghost fire, purge the life of..., in the name of Jesus.

17. Spirit of God overshadow the life of..., in Jesus' name.

18. I decree that ... shall not die but live to declare the works of God, in the name of Jesus.

19. I declare that...shall become a testimony to the society and the family, in the name of Jesus.

20. Every evil hand laid upon.. ., be broken, in the name of Jesus.

21. I shall not bury my children with my hands, in Jesus' name.

22. O God, minister life to my children, in the name of Jesus.

23. Every power of unreasonable behaviour, working against the children, be disgraced, in the name of Jesus.

24. Every power of rebellion targeted at wasting the lives of the children, be dismantled, in the name of Jesus.

25. I bind and cast out from the life of ... (mention the name) the following spirits, in the name of Jesus.

- arrested development
- destructive infirmity
- youthful exuberance
- drug addiction
- sexual immorality
- perversion
- bad company
- alcoholism
- wastage
- untimely death
- self-destruction
- pride
- violence
- murder
- cruelty
- strife
- stubbornness
- rebellion
- anti-social behaviours
- witchcraft
- familiar spirits

# 35

# WOMB POLLUTERS

## INTRODUCTION

These are spirits that hate women with perfect hatred. Their networks and marine spirits pollute the womb with all kinds of infirmities. They are the spirits responsible for many womb problems experienced by women.

## PRAISE WORSHIP

## PRAYER WARFARE

1. I expel from my body every strange material, in Jesus' name.
2. My womb, reject every anti-conception material, in Jesus' name.
3. I uproot every plantation of darkness from my womb, in the name of Jesus.
4. I cut off every negative presence attached to my womb, in the name of Jesus. name.
5. Holy Ghost fire, purge my womb with the blood of Jesus.
6. Blood of Jesus, purge my womb, in the name of Jesus.
7. Every hidden darkness in my womb, be flushed out, in Jesus' name.
8. I push out every plantation of darkness in my womb, in Jesus' name.

9. Every deposit of darkness, loose your hold, in Jesus' name.
10. Every evil hand laid upon my womb, roast, in Jesus' name
11. Anything planted in my womb to drink my blood, come out now, in the name of Jesus.
12. I shall not incubate any property of darkness in my womb, in the name of Jesus.
13. Womb polluters, loose your hold, in the name of Jesus.
14. Anything planted in my life that is contrary to the will of God, be uprooted now, in the name of Jesus.
15. I bind and cast out any dark spirit moving about in my womb, in the name of Jesus,
16. Fire of God, destroy every plantation of infirmity in my womb, in the name of Jesus.
17. Every blood-drinking demon assigned against my womb, I bind and cast you out, in the name of Jesus.
18. Every conspiracy against my vessel of reproduction, be scattered, in the name of Jesus.
19. O God, arise and let every enemy of my marital bliss scatter, in the name of Jesus.
20. My womb, depart from the hold of every altar of darkness, in the name of Jesus.
21. Every burden in my womb, be dissolved, in the name of Jesus.
22. Every yoke in my womb, break, in the name of Jesus.

## STEPS TO PERSONAL DELIVERANCE

***Step ONE*** - Start with praise worship. Praise God with worship songs.

**Step TWO** -Confess out loud Scriptures promising deliverance few of them are: Luke 10:19, E Ephesians 1:7, Romans 16:20, Revelation 12:11, Colossians 2:14, 15, Galatians 3:13,14, Psalm 91:3and 2 Tim, 4:18

**Step THREE** -Break covenants and curses to destroy their legal hold. You can pray a simple prayer: "I break any curse against me"on "I break any covenant against me." A simple prayer with much result

**Step FOUR** -Bind all the spirits associated with those covenants and curses, like this: "I bind all the spirits attached or connected ta the curses and covenants, I have just broken, in the name of Jesus!"

**Step FIVE** - Lay one hand on your head and the other on your stomach or navel and begin to pray like this:"Holy Ghost fire, burn from the top of my head to the soles of my feet." Mention every organ of your body: your kidney, liver, intestines, blood, etc. You must not rush. The fire will actually come and you may start feeling the heat.

**Step SIX**-You begin to saturate yourself with the blood of Jesus. You say: "Blood of Jesus, enter into my spirit, soul and body." Next, you say: "I drink the blood of Jesus, "

**Step 5EVEN** -It is now that you are able to demand firmly, in the name of the Lord Jesus Christ, that any spirit that is not of God, should leave you. You demand it forcefully like this: "In the name of the Lord Jesus Christ, I come against all you hidden spirits and I bind your activities in my life. You can no longer hide below the surface because I now recognize what you have been doing: release me in the name of Jesus." If sickness is the problem, address it and say: "You spirit of infirmity, I speak to you directly, get out of my life now. I am redeemed by the blood of Jesus Christ, come out and go now. out with every breath by the power of the Holy Spirit. I prevail over you,"

At this point, you stop talking: open your mouth and nose and take three to seven deep breaths and expel them forcefully through you mouth and nose. You may be surprised that strange things would beg to happen. Repeat this stage again and again; issue the command, and repeat the breathing in and out.

***Step EIGHT*** - When you have finished the expulsion stage, you ask for a fresh in-filling of the Holy Spirit, and close the session with praises.

Anytime you are attacked in your dream, rise and go through the steps mentioned. It keeps you from becoming sick; it removes every evil seed of the enemy and charges your body with fire. It uproots evil plantations and builds up your confidence.

Every night, before you go to bed, remember these three important prayer points. Pray for the walls of fire to surround you. The Bible says: "For I, saith the Lord, will be unto her a wall of fire round about, and will be the glory in the midst of her."

Two, pray for the blood of Jesus to be upon you. Three, pray that the angels of God should surround you. No matter how sleepy you are, make sure you pray these three prayer points nightly.

# 36

# HELPER MANIPULATORS

## INTRODUCTION

These are spirits that antagonise and manipulate helpers. They initiate situations where a person who desperately needs help does not receive anything. Helpers would break their promises not to suit a person so easily.

## PRAISE WORSHIP

## PRAYER WARFARE

1. You unfriendly helpers, I command you in the name of our Lord Jesus Christ: depart from me.
2. Every spirit antagonising my divine helpers, die, in Jesus' name.
3. Every personality antagonising my divine helpers, die, in the name of Jesus.
4. Every power manipulating my divine helpers against me, die, in the name of Jesus.
5. Every power driving away my God-sent helpers, I command you to die, in the name of Jesus.
6. Father, make all my proposals to find favour in the sight of my divine helpers, in the name of Jesus.
7. Let all the demonic obstacles that have been established in the heart of my divine helpers against my prosperity be destroyed, in the name of Jesus.

8. Let all the demonic obstacles that have been established in the heart of my divine helpers against my destiny be destroyed, in the name of Jesus.
9. Let every satanic siren scaring away my helpers be silenced, in the name of Jesus.
10. I hold the blood of Jesus against lack of good helpers.
11. O Lord, rend the heavens open and bring helpers to me in Your own way.
12. Let my divinely-appointed helpers begin to locate me from now, in the name of Jesus.
13. O Lord, connect me with divine helpers.
14. Every power trying to remove my name from the mind of my helpers, fall down and die now, in the name of Jesus.
15. Every cause of disappearance or unwillingness of would-be helpers in my life, be nullified by the blood of Jesus.
16. Any power creating disfavour and diverting my divinely appointed helpers, be destroyed suddenly, in Jesus' name..
17. Blood of Jesus, wipe away every evil mark upon my life.
18. Let the mark of good favour fall upon me now, in Jesus' name.
19. O God, arise and bring good helpers to me by fire, in Jesus' name.

# 37

# MINISTRY DESTROYERS

## INTRODUCTION

These spirits are enemies of spiritual callings. They focus their attacks on ministers, and ensure that they are either frustrated or eliminated from the ministry. All ministers should learn to deal with these wicked spirits that have destroyed many callings. AlI pastors should constantly pray against these spirits.

**PRAISE WORSHIP**

**Confess Psalms 1 & 2**

**PRAYER WARFARE**

1. Thank the Lord for the privilege of working in His vineyard.
2. Since many are called but few are chosen, thank the Lord for choosing you.
3. Bring quality repentance to the Lord.
4. I shall not be a misfired arrow in the hands of my Maker, in the name of Jesus.
5. Any foundational power working against my calling, be destroyed, in the name of Jesus.
6. Every yoke working against spiritual growth in my life, be broken, in the name of Jesus.

7. The enemy will not make me a bad example, in Jesus' name.
8. Every destructive habit designed to waste my calling, die, in the name of Jesus.
9. Power of good finishing, come upon my destiny, in Jesus' name.
10. Every area of incomplete deliverance in my life, receive complete deliverance by fire, in the name of Jesus.
11. Every spiritual cataract, clear away from my vision, in Jesus' name.
12. Every spirit of slumber, I bury you today, in Jesus' name.
13. The eagle of my calling shall mount up by the power in the blood of Jesus.
14. Every anti-ministry arrow fired into my life, backfire, in the name of Jesus.
15. Holy Ghost fire, destroy all works of darkness in my life, in the name of Jesus.
16. Every door opened to the enemy of my calling, be closed, in the name of Jesus.
17. Let the waters of life flow into every dead area of my spiritual life, in the name of Jesus.
18. Every weapon fashioned against my high calling, be destroyed, in the name of Jesus.
19. Any foundational serpent and scorpion programmed into my life, to destroy my calling in the future, die, in Jesus' name.
20. O God of Elijah, arise and give unto me my mantle of fire, in the name of Jesus.
21. Anything planted within me, that has not manifested now, but will

manifest in future, to make me backslide, dry up, in Jesus' name.

22. Every witchcraft power drinking the blood of my spiritual life, die, in the name of Jesus.
23. Glory of God, overshadow me, in the name of Jesus.
24. Strength of God, empower me, in the name of Jesus.
25. Every internal bondage magnetizing external bondage, be broken, in the name of Jesus.
26. O Glory of my calling, arise and shine, in the name of Jesus.
27. I will not mortgage my calling on the lap of Delilah or Jezebel, in the name of Jesus.
28. I refuse to retire, I must refire, in the name of Jesus.
29. Every enemy of my divine 'well-done' statement at the end of my race, die, in the name of Jesus.
30. My Samson will not be shaven, in the name of Jesus.
31. I receive power to meet the needs of this present generation, in the name of Jesus.
32. All the rough places in my life working against my spiritual breakthroughs, be smoothened by the blood of Jesus.
33. Let Your glory, O Lord, overshadow my destiny, in Jesus' name.
34. I refuse to tarry in the valley of powerlessness, in Jesus' name.
35. I rise above my roots by the power in the blood of Jesus.
36. I declare that I am called by God, no evil power shall cut me down, in the name of Jesus.
37. O Lord, give me power to be faithful to my calling, in Jesus' name.
38. I receive the anointing to remain steady, committed and.

consistent in my ministerial life, in the name of Jesus.

39. I shall not deviate into church politics, church rivalry or rebellion, in the name of Jesus.
40. O Lord, give me the wisdom to respect my teachers and seniors who have trained me, in the name of Jesus.
41. O Lord, give me the heart of a servant, so that I can experience Your blessings everyday, in the name of Jesus.
42. I receive power to mount up with wings as eagles, in Jesus' name.
43. The enemy will not waste my calling, in the name of Jesus.
44. The devil will not swallow my ministerial destiny, in Jesus' name.
45. Power for effective development in my calling: come upon me now, in the name of Jesus.
46. I declare war against spiritual ignorance, in Jesus' name.
47. I bind and cast out every unteachable spirit, in Jesus' name.
48. I receive the anointing for success in my ministry, in Jesus' name.
49, I shall not be an enemy of integrity, in the name of Jesus.
50. I shall not steal God's money, in the name of Jesus.
51, I shall not disgrace the calling of God for my life, in Jesus' name.
52. I shall walk in holiness every day, in the name of Jesus.
53. I bind the spirit of sexual immorality, in the name of Jesus.
54. I receive the culture of loyalty in my ministry, in Jesus' name.
55. I shall not become an old king that is resistant to advice, in the name of Jesus.
56. I shall not live a wasteful and extravagant life, in Jesus' name.
57. I shall not serve my wonderful Saviour for filthy financial gain, in

the name of Jesus.

58. I bind every spirit of quarrel and opposition from my husband/wife, in the name of Jesus.
59. My husband/wife shall not scatter my church members, in the name of Jesus.
60. Every Judas in my ministry, fall into your own trap, in Jesus' name.
61. My ministry will not destroy my marriage, in Jesus name.
62. My marriage will not destroy my ministry, in Jesus' name.
63. My children will not be misfired arrows in my ministry, in the name of Jesus.
64. I claim progress and excellence for my ministry, in Jesus' name.
65. My church shall experience prosperity, in the name of Jesus.
66. O Lord, let my ministry reach the unreached, in Jesus' name.
67. Multitudes will go to heaven because of my ministry, in Jesus' name.
68. I kill every attack on my ministry: I shall prevail, in Jesus' name.
69. I shall not bite the fingers that fed me, in Jesus' name.
70. I shall not engage in rebellion, in the name of Jesus.
71. Every power of my father's house working against my calling, die, in the name of Jesus.
72. Anointing for excellence, fall upon me, in the name of Jesus.
73. Lord, break me and re-mould me, in the name of Jesus.
74. I will not surrender to the enemy, in the name of Jesus.
75. I shall not die before my time, in the name of Jesus.

76. I shall not capture the prosperity of Naaman, in Jesus' name.
77. Let God arise and let every enemy of my calling scatter, in the name of Jesus.
78. I receive fresh fire and fresh anointing, in Jesus' name.
79. Holy fire of revival, fall upon my branch, in Jesus' name.

# 38
# SPIRIT OF JEZEBEL

## INTRODUCTION

**Rev. 2:20:** Notwithstanding I have a few things against thee, because thou sufferest that woman Jezebel, which calleth herself a prophetess, to teach and to seduce my servants to commit fornication, and to eat things sacrificed unto idols.

This is an oppressive, dominating, manipulating and wicked spirit. It hates true prophets of God and is determined to kill them. It strives to undermine God's order for the home.

**PRAISE WORSHIP**

**PRAYER WARFARE**

1. I attack and bury every power of Jezebel, in Jesus' name.
2. I take away all the known and unknown powers of Jezebel's titles, in the name of Jesus.
3. Every power of the mistress of sorcery and witchcraft, be dismantled, in the name of Jesus.
4. Every cord of Jezebel, break, in the name of Jesus.
5. Every magical operation of Jezebel, be destroyed, in Jesus' name.
6. All Jezebel veils of magic, scatter, in Jesus' name.

7. I bring the scare and vengeance of the Lord upon every Jezebelian power assigned against me, in Jesus' name.
8. All curses of Jezebel, break, in the name of Jesus.
9. Every evil soul-tie with Jezebel spirit, break, in Jesus' name.
10. Every door opened by Jezebel spirit, be closed, in Jesus' name.
11. I attack and destroy all areas of control held by Jezebel, in the name of Jesus.
12. Quenchers of deliverance, die, in the name of Jesus.
13. I cancel all plans and programmes of Jezebel, in Jesus' name.
14. I de-programme every Jezebel spirit and cancel its assignment, in the name of Jesus.
15. Every spirit of Jezebel, manifest and come out, in Jesus' name.
16. I bind the powers of Jezebel and separate them from my life, in the name of Jesus.
17. I execute judgement on Jezebel and her house, in Jesus' name.
18. I bind the spirit of Jezebel in any area of my life and I command it to come out, in the name of Jesus.
19. I bind and cast out every spirit of Jezebel delegated against me, in the name of Jesus.
20. I pull down the stronghold of Jezebel in my life, in Jesus' name.
21. Oh Lord, anoint me specially to deal with the spirit of Jezebel in my family.
22. Every evil seed sown by the spirit of Jezebel in my life, die, in the name of Jesus.
23. Holy Ghost fire, overhaul my existence, in Jesus' name.

24. O Lord, make me Your battle axe, to destroy the works of the spirit of Jezebel, in the name of Jesus.
25. You spirit of Jezebel and your cohorts, loose your hold over my life, in the name of Jesus.
26. O Lord, forgive me for the root of Jezebel in my life and character.
27. Every curse of Jezebel upon my destiny, break, in Jesus' name
28. I receive the power to throw down every Jezebel in my life, in the name of Jesus.
29. Every opposition of the strongholds of Jezebel against my open door to the mansions of glory, die, in Jesus' name.
30. O Lord, help me so that the strongholds of Jezebel will not make me to loose my second chance, in the name of Jesus.
31. Every witchcraft altar erected by the spirit of Ahab against my family, scatter, in the name of Jesus.
32. I challenge the spirit of Ahab in the foundation of my life by fire., in the name of Jesus.
33. Every spell of Jezebel on my life, break, in Jesus' name.
34. Holy fire of God, separate me from all evil congregations, in the name of Jesus.
35. I overcome by the blood of Jesus, every doctrine of the spirit of Jezebel, in Jesus' name.
36. Every presence of witchcraft in my family, disappear today by the blood of Jesus.
37. O God of Elijah destroy every Jezebelian spirit in my life, in the name of Jesus

38. Blood of Jesus, purge my life of every seed of Jezebel.
39. I pull down every activity of the spirit of Jezebel in my life and family, in the name of Jesus.
40. Thou power of Jezebel of my father's house, die, in Jesus' name.
41. Thou power of Jezebel of my mother's house, die, in Jesus' name
42. O Lord, let me be crucified with You, in the name of Jesus.

# 39

# SPIRIT OF SLUMBER

## INTRODUCTION

Romans 11:8 (According as it is written, God hath given them the spirit of slumber, eyes that they should not see, and ears that they should not hear:) unto this day.

Isaiah 29: 40: For the LORD hath poured out upon
sleep, and hath closed your eyes: the prophets and your rulers, the seers hath he covered.

This is the spirit responsible for spiritual drowsiness and dullness. Blindness and deafness then follow this leading to physical or spiritual death. Victims experience sleeping more than usual, insomnia and mental inertness; falling asleep while reading the Bible only, is a trademark.

## PRAISE WORSHIP

## PRAYER WARFARE

1. O God, arise and deliver me from every spirit of the valley, in the name of Jesus,
2. Every power weighing down my spirit-man, be unseated, in the

3. Every power affecting my worship for God, be dismantled, in the name of Jesus.
4. Every power of spiritual stagnation, die, in Jesus' name.
5. Every spirit of drowsiness and slumber, loose your hold, in the name of Jesus.
6. Holy Ghost fire, incubate my spirit-man with Your revival spirit, in the name of Jesus.
7. Let my inner man receive the fire of God to move forward, in the name of Jesus.
8. Every power of confusion overshadowing my spirit-man, scatter, in the name of Jesus.
9. I refuse to be a student in the school of spiritual sleep, in the name of Jesus.
10 Every power targeting my spirit-man for destruction, be dismantled, in the name of Jesus.
11. Let the chariot of war arise from the throne of God, and disband every arrow of laziness in my life, in Jesus' name.
12 Spirit of revival, come upon me, in the name of Jesus.
13. Holy Ghost fire, purge my spirit-man, in the name of Jesus.
14. I receive fresh fire from the altar of God to press on, in the name of Jesus.
15. I receive deliverance from every satanic technology targeted at my spiritual life, in the name of Jesus.
16. O God, have mercy on me and deliver me from every form of lukewarmness, in the name of Jesus.
17. Every evil sleep that endangers my destiny, be wiped off, in the name of Jesus.

18. Any satanic animal programmed into my life to affect my spiritual life, die, in the name of Jesus.
19. Every yoke of slumber and deep evil sleep, melt away, in the name of Jesus.
20. Every arrow of discouragement and confusion, be neutralised, in the name of Jesus.
21. I shall not die but live to declare the works of God, in Jesus' name
22. I release myself from every ancestral demonic pollution, in the name of Jesus.
23. I release myself from every demonic pollution emanating from my parents' religion, in the name of Jesus.
24. I release myself from demonic pollution emanating from my past involvement in any demonic religion, in Jesus' name.
25. I break and loose myself from every idol and related association, in the name of Jesus.
26. I release myself from every dream pollution, in Jesus' name.
27. Let every satanic attack on my life in my dreams be converted to victory, in the name of Jesus.
28. Let all rivers, trees, forests, evil companions, evil pursuers, pictures of dead relatives, snakes, spirit husbands, spirit wives and masquerades manipulated against me in the dream, be completely destroyed by the power in the blood of the Lord Jesus
29. I command every evil plantation in my life: Come out with all your roots, in the name of Jesus! *(Lay your hands on your stomach and keep repeating the emphasised area.)*

30. Evil strangers in my body, come all the way out of your hiding places, in the name of Jesus.
31. I disconnect any conscious or unconscious linkage with demonic caterers, in the name of Jesus.
32. Let all avenues of eating or drinking spiritual poisons, be closed, in the name of Jesus.
33. I cough out and vomit any food eaten from the table of the devil, in the name of Jesus. (Cough it out and vomit it by faith. Prime the expulsion.)
34. Let all negative materials circulating in my blood stream be evacuated, in the name of Jesus.
35. I drink the blood of Jesus. (Physically swallow it by faith. Do this for some time.).
36. *Lay one hand on your head and the other on your stomach or navel and pray like this:* Holy Ghost Fire, burn from the top of my head to the soles of my feet. Mention every organ of your body: your kidney, liver, intestines, blood, etc. You must not rush. The fire will actually come and you may start feeling the heat.
37. I cut myself off every spirit of . .. *(mention the name of your place of birth)*, in the name of Jesus.
38. I cut myself off every tribal spirit and curse, in Jesus' name.
39. I cut myself off every territorial spirit and curses, in Jesus' name.
40. Holy Ghost Fire, purge my life.
41. I claim my complete deliverance, in the name of Jesus, from the spirit of ... *(mention those things you do not desire in your life)*.
42. I break the hold of any evil power over my life, in Jesus' name.

## 40

## SPIRIT OF INFIRMITY

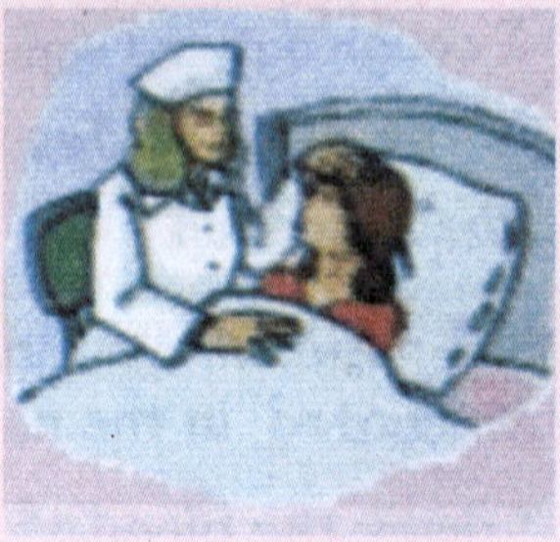

### INTRODUCTION

**Luke 13:11;** And, behold, there was a woman which had a spirit of infirmity eighteen years, and was bowed together, and could in no wise lift up herself. This is the spirit responsible for disease, unwholeness and sickness. This spirit always has the agenda to terminate life, if not arrested. There is practically a spirit behind every disease.

### PRAISE WORSHIP

### PRAYER WARFARE

1. Confession of sins.
2. I command every evil plantation in my life: Come out with all their roots, in the name of Jesus! *(Lay your hands on your stomach and keep repeating the emphasized area)*
3. I cough out and vomit any food eaten from the table of the devil, in the name of Jesus. *(Cough it out and vomit it by faith. Prime the expulsion)*
4. Let all negative materials circulating in my blood stream, be evacuated, in the name of Jesus.
5. I drink the blood of Jesus. *(Physically swallow by faith. Do this for some time.)*

6. Lay one hand on your head and the other on your stomach or navel and begin to pray like this:"Holy Ghost fire, burn from the top of my head to the sole of my feet." Mention every organ of your body: your kidney, liver, intestines, blood, etc. You must not rush. The fire will actually come and you may start feeling the heat.
7. Let the blood of Jesus be transfused into my blood vessels, in the name of Jesus
8. I command every agent of disease in my blood and body organs to die, in the name of Jesus.
9. Let my blood reject every evil foreign entity, in Jesus' name.
10. Holy Spirit, speak deliverance and healing into my life, in the name of Jesus.
11. Let the blood of Jesus speak disappearance unto every infirmity in my life.
12. I hold the blood of Jesus against you spirit of .... (mention what is troubling you). You have to flee.
13. O Lord, let Your healing hand be stretched out upon my life now
14. O Lord, let Your miracle hand be stretched out upon my life now.
15. O Lord, let Your deliverance hand be stretched out upon my life now.
16. I break up every engagement with the spirit of death, in Jesus' name.
17. I rebuke every refuge of sickness, in the name of Jesus.
18. I destroy the grip and operation of sickness upon my life, in the name of Jesus.
19. Every knee of infirmity in my life, bow, in the name of Jesus,
20. O Lord, let my negativity be converted to positivity.

21. I command death upon any sickness in any area of my life, in the name of Jesus.
22. I shall see my sickness no more, in the name of Jesus.
23. Father Lord, let the whirlwind of God scatter every vessel of infirmity fashioned against my life, in the name of Jesus.
24. Every spirit hindering my perfect healing,. fall down and die now, in the name of Jesus.
25. Father Lord, let all death contractors begin to kill themselves, in the name of Jesus.
26. Father Lord, let every germ of infirmity in my body die, in the name of Jesus.
27. Father Lord, let every agent of sickness working against my health disappear, in the name of Jesus.
28 Fountain of discomfort in my life, dry up now, in Jesus' name.
29. Every dead organ in my body, receive life now, in Jesus' name.
30. Father Lord, let my blood be transfused with the blood of Jesus to effect my perfect health, in the name of Jesus
31. Every internal disorder, receive order, in Jesus' name.
32. Every infirmity, come out with all your roots, in Jesus' name.
33. I withdraw every conscious and unconscious cooperation with sickness, in the name of Jesus.
34. O Lord, let the whirlwind of God blow away every wind of infirmity.
35. I release my body from every curse of infirmity, in Jesus' name.
36. O Lord, let the blood of Jesus flush every evil deposit out of my blood.
37. I recover every organ of my body from every evil altar, in

Jesus' name.

38. I withdraw my body from the manipulation of every caldron of darkness, in the name of Jesus.

39. Holy Ghost fire, destroy every stubborn agent of disease in my body, in the name of Jesus.

40. I arrest every demon of terminal disease, in Jesus' name.

41. I cancel every clinical prophecy concerning my life, in Jesus' name.

42. Holy Ghost fire, boil every infirmity out of my system, in the name of Jesus.

43. I cancel every witchcraft verdict for my life, in Jesus' name.

44. O earth, vomit anything that has been buried inside you against my health, in the name of Jesus.

45. Every tree that infirmity has planted in my blood, be uprooted by fire, in the name of Jesus.

46. I command every witchcraft arrow to depart from my
- spinal cord - spleen - navel - heart
- throat, in the name of Jesus.

47. I bind every evil present in my body system, in the name of Jesus. (Mention every organ of your body: your) - excretory
- reproductive - digestive - respiratory - nervous
- skeletal - muscular - circulatory - endocrine

48. I break the backbone and destroy the root of every spirit speaking against me, in the name of Jesus.

49. Thank God for your healing.

# 41

## SPIRIT OF JEALOUSY

### INTRODUCTION

**Numbers 5:14:** And the spirit of jealousy come upon him, and he be jealous of his wife, and she be defiled: or if the spirit of jealousy come upon him, and he be jealous of his wife, and she be not defiled:

The spirit of jealousy ignites hard feelings of envy and resentment. It fires the victim with deadly passions and opens the door to other wicked spirits.

**PRAISE WORSHIP**

**PRAYER WARFARE**

1. Blood of Jesus, avail for me in every department of my life.
2. I close down every entry point of the spirit of jealousy into my life, in the name of Jesus.
3. Every ladder of sexual defilement magnetizing spirit of jealousy. be dismantled, in the name of Jesus.
4. I bind and cast out every inherited spirit of jealousy, in the name of Jesus.
5. Every demonic entry point of anger, be closed, in Jesus' name.
6. I forgive all who have offended me one way or the other, in the

name of Jesus.

7. Every root of bitterness in my life dry up and die, in Jesus' name.
8. Holy Ghost fire, purge my life, in the name of Jesus.
9. I refuse to be a candidate of satanic manipulation, in Jesus' name.
10. O God, arise and let every spiritual filthiness in my life scatter, in the name of Jesus.
11. Every yoke of envy and jealousy, break, in Jesus' name.
12. I release myself from every bitter memory of the past, in the name of Jesus.
13. By the power in the blood of Jesus, I pull down every stronghold of resentment and hatred, in the name of Jesus.
14. I refuse to be hooked to offences, in the name of Jesus.
15. Spirit of the living God, arise with Your weapons of war and fill my heart with Your love, in the name of Jesus.
16. Any problem brought into my life through the doorway of jealousy, be dismantled, in the name of Jesus.
17. I shall arise above negative circumstances seeking to pull me down, in the name of Jesus.
18. Thou yoke of the oppressor, hanging around my neck, be broken, in the name of Jesus.
19. Every lion of jealousy devouring my breakthrough, die, in the name of Jesus.
20. Lord Jesus, hold my hand and lead me away from every path of envy, in the name of Jesus.
21. Let the fruit of the Spirit manifest mightily in my life, in the name of Jesus.

22. I receive the power to destroy every arrow of jealousy, in the name of Jesus.
23. My life, receive the fire that kills bitterness, in Jesus' name.
24. O Lord, deliver me from every trap of jealousy, in Jesus' name.
25. I shall not be a prey in the mouth of any spirit of hell, in the name of Jesus.

# 42

# FAMILIAR SPIRITS

## INTRODUCTION

Deut. 18;:10: There shall not be found among you any one that maketh his son or his daughter to pass through the fire, or that useth divination, or an observer of times, or an enchanter, or a witch,

These are secretive spirits that are familiar with their victims. They bring evil to the surface and supervise inherited evil patterns.

## PRAISE WORSHIP

## PRAYER WARFARE

1. Let the power of God destroy every foundation of familiar spirits in my family, in the name of Jesus. Thou foundation of familiar spirits in my father's house / mother's house, die, in Jesus' name.
2. Let every soul-tie with familiar spirits be broken to pieces, in the name of Jesus.
3. Every seat of familiar spirits, receive the thunder fire of God, in the name of Jesus.
4. Let the habitation of familiar spirits be desolate, in Jesus' name.
5. Every throne of familiar spirits, be dismantled by fire, in the name of Jesus.

6. Let the stronghold of familiar spirits be pulled down by fire, in the name of Jesus.
7. Let the diviners of familiar spirits be rendered impotent, in Jesus' name.
8. Let the network of familiar spirits be dismantled, in Jesus' name.
9. Let the communication systems of familiar spirits be destroyed by fire, in the name of Jesus.
10. Every transportation system of familiar spirits, be disrupted, in the name of Jesus.
11 Let the weapons of the familiar spirits turn against them, in the name of Jesus.
12. I withdraw my blessings from every bank or strongroom of familiar spirits, in the name of Jesus.
13. O altar of familiar spirits, break, in the name of Jesus.
14. Every familiar spirits' padlock fashioned against me, break by fire, in the name of Jesus.
15. Every trap of familiar spirits, roast by the fire of God, in the name of Jesus.
16. Every familiar spirits' utterance and projection made against me, be overthrown, in the name of Jesus,
17. I reverse every familiar spirit's burial fashioned against me, in the name of Jesus.
18. I deliver my soul from every bewitchment of familiar spirit, in the name of Jesus,
19. I reverse the effect of every summon of my spirit by familiar spirits, in the name of Jesus.

20. Every familiar spirits' identification mark, be wiped off by the blood of Jesus.
21. I frustrate every familiar spirits' exchange of my virtues, in the name of Jesus.
22. Let the blood of Jesus destroy every familiar spirits' manipulation fashioned against me in the name of Jesus.
23. Let every spell and enchantment programmed against me by familiar spirits be destroyed, in the name of Jesus.
24. Every covenant with familiar spirits, melt by the blood of Jesus.
25. I withdraw every organ of my body from any altar of familiar spirits, in the name of Jesus.
26. Anything planted in my life by familiar spirits, come out now and die, in the name of Jesus.
27. Let the blood of Jesus cancel every initiation of familiar spirits against my destiny, in the name of Jesus.
28. Every spiritual marriage with familiar spirits, be destroyed, in the name of Jesus.
29. I reverse every evil pattern of familiar spirits for my destiny, in the name of Jesus.
30. Every cage of familiar spirits caging my life, be destroyed, in the name of Jesus.

# 43

# WITCHCRAFT SPIRITS

## INTRODUCTION

One of the greatest strongholds confronting believers is the spirit of witchcraft. It is the spirit of manipulation and control. A witch is a person who uses magic for evil purposes or who practises sorcery. A sorcerer is someone who practises magic with the help of evil spirits. Witches excel in wickedness. Occult practice is enhanced by the power of witchcraft.

## PRAISE WORSHIP

## PRAYER WARFARE

1. O Rock of Ages, smash to pieces every foundation of witchcraft in my family, in the name of Jesus. Thou foundation of witchcraft in my father's house/ mother's house, die, in the name of Jesus.
2. Let witchcraft powers eat their own flesh and drink their own blood, in the name of Jesus.
3. Every seat of witchcraft, receive the thunder fire of God, in the name of Jesus.
4. Let the habitation of witchcraft powers be desolate, in the name of Jesus.
5. Every throne of witchcraft, be dismantled by fire, in Jesus' name.

6 Let the stronghold of witchcraft powers be pulled down by fire, in the name of Jesus.

7. Let the refuge of witchcraft be disgraced, in Jesus' name.

8. Let the network of witchcraft disintegrate, in Jesus' name.

9. Let the communication systems of witchcraft powers be destroyed by fire, in the name of Jesus.

10. Every transportation system of witchcraft powers, be disrupted, in the name of Jesus.

11. Let the weapons of witchcraft powers turn against them, in the name of Jesus.

12. I withdraw my blessings from every bank or strongroom of the enemy, in the name of Jesus.

13. O altar of witchcraft, break, in the name of Jesus.

14. Every witchcraft padlock fashioned against me, break by fire, in the name of Jesus.

15. Every trap of witchcraft, catch your owners, in Jesus' name.

16. Every witchcraft utterance and projection made against me, be overthrown, in the name of Jesus.

17. I reverse every witchcraft burial fashioned against me, in the name of Jesus.

18. I deliver my soul from every witchcraft bewitchment, in the name of Jesus.

19. I reverse the effect of every witchcraft summoning of my spirit, in the name of Jesus.

20. Every witchcraft identification mark, be wiped off by the blood of Jesus.

21. I frustrate every witchcraft exchange of my virtues, in the name of Jesus.

22. Let the blood of Jesus block the flying route of witchcraft powers targeted against me.

23. Let every witchcraft curse break and be destroyed, in Jesus' name.

24. Every covenant of witchcraft, melt by the blood of Jesus.

25. I withdraw every organ of my body from any witchcraft altar in the name of Jesus.

26. Anything planted in my life by witchcraft, come out now and die, in the name of Jesus.

27. Let the blood of Jesus cancel every witchcraft initiation fashioned against my destiny, in the name of Jesus.

28. Every witchcraft poison, be destroyed, in the name of Jesus.

29. I reverse every witchcraft pattern fashioned against my destiny, in the name of Jesus.

30. Every witchcraft cage fashioned against my life, be destroyed, in the name of Jesus.

31. Let every problem in my life that originated from witchcraft, receive divine and instant solution, in Jesus' name.

32. I command all the damages done to my life by witchcraft to be repaired, in the name of Jesus.

33. Let every blessing confiscated by witchcraft spirits be released, in Jesus' name.

34. Every witchcraft power assigned against my life and marriage, receive. .. (pick from the under listed), in the name of Jesus.

- the thunder and lightning of God
- hail and fire mingled with the blood of the Lamb
- unbearable heat
- concentrated acid
- destroying flood
- destruction
- raging fire
- continuous plagues
- failure
- confusion

35. I loose myself from any power of witchcraft, in Jesus' name.
36. Every camp of witchcraft gathered against my prosperity, fall down and die, in Jesus' name.
37. Every witchcraft pot working against me, I bring the judgment of God against you, in the name of Jesus.
38. I command every witchcraft pot using remote control against my health to be broken into pieces, in Jesus' name.
39. Witchcraft opposition, receive the rain of affliction, in the name of Jesus.
40. Let the spirit of witchcraft attack the familiar spirits fashioned against me, in Jesus' name.
41. I retrieve my integrity out of the hands of household witchcraft, in the name of Jesus.
42. I break the power of the occult, witchcraft and familiar spirits over my life, in Jesus' name.
43. In the name of Jesus, I break and loose myself from all evil Curses, chains, spells, jinxes, bewitchments, witchcraft or sorcery which may have been put upon me.
44. Let the thunder of God locate and dismantle the throne of witchcraft in my household, in the name of Jesus.

45. Let every seat of witchcraft in my household be roasted by the fire of God, in Jesus' name.

46. Let the altar of witchcraft in my household be roasted, in the name of Jesus.

47. Let the thunder of God scatter beyond redemption, the foundation of witchcraft in my household, in Jesus' name.

48. Every stronghold of refuge of my household witches, be destroyed, in the name of Jesus.

49. Every hiding place and secret place of witchcraft in my family, be exposed by fire, in the name of Jesus.

50. Let every local and international witchcraft network of my household witches be shattered to pieces, in Jesus' name.

51. Let the communication system of my household witches be frustrated, in the name of Jesus.

52. Let the terrible fire of God consume the transportation of my household witchcraft, in the name of Jesus.

53. Every agent ministering at the altar of witchcraft in my household, fall down and die, in the name of Jesus.

54. Let the thunder and the fire of God locate the storehouses and strongrooms of the household witchcraft harbouring my blessings, and pull them down, in the name of Jesus.

55. Let any witchcraft curses working against me be revoked by the blood of Jesus.

56. Every decision, vow and covenant of household witchcraft affecting me, be nulified by the blood of Jesus.

57. I destroy with the fire of God, every weapon of witchcraft used

against me, in Jesus' name.

58. Any material taken from my body and now placed on a witchcraft altar, be roasted by the fire of God, in the name of Jesus.

59. I reverse every witchcraft burial fashioned against me, in the name of Jesus.

60. Every trap set for me by witches, begin to catch your owners, in the name of Jesus.

61. Every witchcraft padlock fashioned against any area of my life, be roasted, in Jesus' name.

62. Let the wisdom of household witches be converted to foolishness, in the name of Jesus.

63. Let the wickedness of household enemies overtake them, in the name of Jesus.

64. I deliver my soul from every witchcraft bewitchment, in the name of Jesus.

65. Any witchcraft bird flying for my sake, fall down, die and be roasted to ashes, in the name of Jesus.

66. Any of my blessings traded with by household witches, be returned to me, in Jesus' name.

67. Any of my blessings and testimonies swallowed by witches, be converted to hot coals of fire of God and be vomited, in the name of Jesus.

68. I break myself loose from every bondage of witchcraft covenants, in the name of Jesus.

69. Any witchcraft coven where any of my blessings are hidden, be roasted by the fire of God, in the name of Jesus.

70. (Lay your right hand on your head) Every witchcraft spirit plantation, pollution, deposit and material in my body, melt by the fire of God and be flushed out by the blood of Jesus.

71. Every evil, ever done to me through witchcraft attack, be reversed, in the name of Jesus.

72. Every witchcraft hand planting evil seeds in my life through dream attacks, wither and burn to ashes, in Jesus' name.

73. Every witchcraft obstacle put on the road to my desired miracle and success, be removed by the east wind of God, in Jesus' name.

74. Every witchcraft chant, spell and projection made against me, I bind you and turn you against your owner, in Jesus' name.

75. I frustrate every plot, device, scheme and project of witchcraft designed to affect any area of my life, in the name of Jesus.

76. Any witch projecting himself into the body of any animal in order to do me harm, be trapped in the body of such an animal forever, in the name of Jesus.

77. Any drop of my blood sucked by any witch, be vomited now, in the name of Jesus.

78. Any part of me shared out amongst household/village witches, I recover you, in the name of Jesus.

79. Any organ of my body that has been exchanged for another through witchcraft operation, be replaced now, in Jesus' name

80. I recover any of my virtues/blessings shared out amongst village / household witches, in the name of Jesus.

81. I reverse the evil effect of any witchcraft invocation or summoning of my spirit, in the name of Jesus.

82 I loose my hands and feet from any witchcraft bewitchment or bondage, in Jesus' name.

83 Let the blood of Jesus wash away every witchcraft identification mark on me or on any of my properties, in Jesus' name.

84. I forbid any re-union or re-gathering of household and village witches against my life, in the name of Jesus.

85. Let the entire body system of my household witches begin to run amok until they confess all their wickedness, in Jesus' name.

86. Let the mercies of God be withdrawn from them, in Jesus' name.

87. Let them begin to grope in the daytime as in the thickness of a dark night, in the name of Jesus.

88. Let everything that has ever worked for them begin to work against them, in Jesus' name.

89. Let them not have a cloth to cover their shame, in Jesus' name.

90. Let as many of them that are stubbornly unrepentant, be smitten by the sun in the day and by the moon in the night, in Jesus' name.

91. Let each step they take lead them to greater destruction, in the name of Jesus.

92. But as for me. let me dwell in the hollow of God's hand, in the name of Jesus.

93. Let the goodness and mercies of God overwhelm me now, in the name of Jesus.

94. Any witchcraft operation under any water against my life, receive immediate judgment of fire, in the name of Jesus.

95. Every witchcraft power, that has introduced spirit husband/wife or child into my dreams, be roasted by fire, in the name of Jesus.

96. Every agent of witchcraft power, posing as my husband/wife or child in my dreams, be roasted by fire, in Jesus' name.

97. Every agent of witchcraft power, physically attached to my marriage to frustrate it, fall down now and perish, in Jesus' name

98. Every agent of witchcraft power, assigned to attack my finances through dream, fall down and perish, in Jesus' name.

99. Let the thunderbolts of God locate and destroy every witchcraft coven, where deliberations and decisions were fashioned against me, in the name of Jesus.

100. Any water spirit from my village or place of birth, practising witchcraft against me and my family, be amputated by the Word of God, in the name of Jesus.

101. Any power of witchcraft, holding any of my blessings in bondage, receive the fire of God and release them, in the name of Jesus.

102 I loose my mind and soul, from the bondage of marine witches, in the name of Jesus.

103, Any witchcraft power chain, binding my hands and feet from prospering, be shattered to pieces, in Jesus' name.

104. Every arrow, shot into my life from under any water through witchcraft, come out of me and go back to your sender, in the name of Jesus.

105. Any evil material, transferred into my body through contact with any witchcraft agent, roast by fire, in the name of Jesus.

106. Any evil, done against me through witchcraft oppression or manipulation, be reversed by the blood of Jesus.

107 I bind every witchcraft control and mind-blinding spirit, in the name of Jesus.

108. I cast out every witchcraft arrow affecting my senses (sight., smell, taste, hearing), in the name of Jesus.

109. I command every witchcraft arrow to depart from my
 - spinal cord - spleen - navel - heart - throat
 - eyes - head

110. Let the blood of Jesus purge me of every witchcraft contaminating material, in the name of Jesus.

111. I destroy the hand of any witch-doctor working against me, in the name of Jesus.

112. Every witchcraft spirit attempting to build a wall against my destiny, fall down and die, in the name of Jesus.

113. I send the rain of affliction upon every witchcraft power working against me, in the name of Jesus.

114. O sun, moon, stars, earth, water and the elements, vomit every enchantment that is against me, in the name of Jesus

115. Every power using the heavenlies against me, fall down and be disgraced, in Jesus' name.

116. Let the stars of heaven begin to fight for me, in Jesus' name.

117. O God, arise and scatter every conspiracy in the heavenlies that is against me, in Jesus' name.

118. I break with the blood of Jesus all evil soul-ties affecting my life, in the name of Jesus.

119. Spirit of the living God, come upon my life and place a shield of protection around me, in the name of Jesus.

120. Every chain of inherited witchcraft in my family, break, in the name of Jesus.

121. Every ladder used by witchcraft against me, be roasted, in the name of Jesus.

122. Any door that I have opened to witchcraft in any area of my life, be closed for ever by the blood of Jesus.

123. I revoke every witchcraft verdict on my marital life, in the name of Jesus.

124. I send confusion into the camp of household witchcraft, in the name of Jesus.

125. Stubborn witchcraft, release me, in the name of Jesus.

126. Every witchcraft power working against my destiny, fall down and die, in Jesus' name.

127. Every incantation, ritual and witchcraft power against my destiny, fall down and die, in the name of Jesus.

128. I break the power of the occult, witchcraft and familiar spirits over my life, in Jesus' name.

129. Witchcraft opposition, receive the rain of affliction, in the name of Jesus.

130, I cancel every witchcraft verdict against my life, in Jesus' name.

131. I command every arrow of witchcraft in my life: Come out with all your roots in the name of Jesus! (Lay your hands on your stomach and pray aggressively.)

132, I command every witchcraft pot using remote control against my health to be broken into pieces, in Jesus' name.

133. I rebuke the spell of any witchcraft pot from my neck, in the name of Jesus.

134. I break every witchcraft pot over my life, in Jesus'

135. Every council of witchcraft working against me will not prosper, in the name of Jesus.

136. I disentangle myself and my family from every witchcraft cage and pot, in the name of Jesus.

137 I retrieve my integrity from the hands of household witchcraft, in the name of Jesus,

138. Every witchcraft hand planting evil seeds in my life through dream attacks, wither and burn to ashes, in Jesus' name.

139. Let all friendly witchcraft powers be exposed and disgraced, in the name of Jesus.

140. O Lord, plant Your warring angels around me to dismantle and destroy evil stronghold of internal witchcraft.

141. I exercise my authority over stubborn witchcraft and I pull down its structures, in Jesus' name.

142. Every placental witchcraft, targeted against my destiny, what are you waiting for? Die, in the name of Jesus.

143. Placental witchcraft, manipulating my destiny, die, in Jesus' name

144. Every blessing that I have lost through placental witchcraft, I repossess you, in Jesus' name.

145. Every witchcraft coven and marine banks, release my placenta, in Jesus' name

146. Every cage of family witchcraft, release my divine partner, in Jesus' name.

147. Oh Lord, let my dreams and visions, reject every witchcraft projection, in the name of Jesus.

148. Thank God for answers to your prayers.

# 44 WICKED SPIRITS

## INTRODUCTION

**Ephes. 6:12:** For we wrestle not against flesh and blood, but against principalities, against powers, against the rulers of the darkness of this world, against spiritual wickedness in high places.

**Matthew 11:12:** And from the days of John the Baptist until now the kingdom of heaven suffereth violence, and the violent take it by force.

These are wicked spirits resident in the three spiritual strongholds, i.e., the heavenlies, the earth and the sea. They are mercilessly destructive. They destroy the body, the soul, the spirit, destinies, environments and ministries.

**PRAISE WORSHIP**

**PRAYER WARFARE**

1. Let all the wicked spirits around me, fall by their own wickedness, in the name of Jesus.
2. You harmful, hereditary and other wicked spirits, loose your hold

over my life, in the name of Jesus.

3. I seize power from every wicked spirit militating against my life, in the name of Jesus.

4. I declare that satan and his wicked spirits are under my feet, in the name of Jesus.

5. Every wicked spirit planning to rob me of the will of God, fall down and die, in the name of Jesus.

6. Every familiar and wicked spirit behind my situation, get out of my life, in the name of Jesus.

7. Let the wicked spirits polluting the hearts of my helpers against me, receive the stones of fire, in the name of Jesus.

8. I bring the blood of Jesus over every evidence that can be tendered by wicked spirits against me, in the name of Jesus.

9. Every internal warfare in my life, quench, in Jesus' name

10, Every warfare in the heavenlies prepared against my peace, I command panic upon you, in the name of Jesus.

11. Every warfare prepared by wicked spirits against my peace, command havoc upon you, in the name of Jesus.

12. Every warfare prepared by wicked spirits against my marriage, I command chaos upon you, in the name of Jesus.

13. Every warfare prepared by wicked spirits against my finances, I command pandemonium upon you, in the name of Jesus.

14. Every warfare prepared by wicked spirits against my destiny, I command disaster upon you, in Jesus' name.

15. Every warfare prepared by wicked spirits against my calling, I command confusion upon you, in Jesus' name.

16. Every warfare prepared by wicked spirits against my family line, I command spiritual acid upon you, in Jesus' name.
17. Every warfare in the earth, prepared by wicked spirits against my peace, I command destruction upon you, in the name of Jesus.
18. Every warfare in the sea prepared by wicked spirits against my peace, I command hornets of the Lord upon you, in Jesus' name.
19. Every warfare prepared by wicked spirits against my progress, I command brimstone and hailstone upon you, in the name of Jesus.
20. I bind and cast out, every power causing internal warfare, in the name of Jesus.
21. O God, arise and scatter every camp of wicked spirits fashioned against me, in the name of Jesus.

# 45

# SPIRIT OF ERROR

## INTRODUCTION

1 John 4:6: We are of God: he that knoweth God heareth us: he that is not of God heareth not us. Hereby know we the spirit of truth, and the spirit of error.

Spirit of error is the spirit that leads people astray. It diverts people away from the truth. It is the author of repeated mistakes and all who have hatred for perfection, correction and honesty are its victims.

## PRAISE WORSHIP

## PRAYER WARFARE

1. I bind and cast out every spirit of error, in Jesus' name.
2. I declare that I am not a victim of any spirit of error, in the name of Jesus.
3. I rise above all chains of unpardonable mistakes, in Jesus' name.
4. Let my life be released from the chains of deception, in the name of Jesus.
5. I destroy every satanic manipulation of my destiny, in Jesus' name.
6. Holy Ghost, disconnect my life from every satanic agenda, in the name of Jesus,

7. I pull down every stronghold of error, in the name of Jesus.

8. Power of God, deliver me from evil diversion, in Jesus' name.

9. Every gate of brass and bars of iron of error, break, in the name of Jesus.

9. Prayer Warfare Against 70 Mad Spirits 186

10. Fire of God, burn to ashes every programme of error for my life, in the name of Jesus.

11. I shall not repeat the error of my father's house, in Jesus' name.

12. Every power of low-profile life, die, in the name of Jesus.

13. I remove my life from every journey into darkness, in the name of Jesus.

14. My spirit man, reject every arrow of error, in Jesus' name.

15. I go from strength to strength, and from glory to glory, in the name of Jesus.

16. Let my way be clear and plain before me, in Jesus' name.

17. Every power introducing error into my life, die, in Jesus' name.

18. I reject the power of the tail, in the name of Jesus.

19. I disconnect myself from spiritual cobweb, in Jesus' name.

20. I drink the blood of Jesus.

21. Glory of God, overshadow my life, in the name of Jesus.

# 46

# ANTI-CHRIST SPIRIT

## INTRODUCTION

**1 John 4:6:** We are of God: he that knoweth God heareth us; he that is not of God heareth not us. Hereby know we the spirit of truth, and the spirit of error.

The anti-Christ spirit works against Christ. It sponsors false doctrines, prophecies, teachings and blasphemies. It aims at making men believe that they do not need the Saviour. The spirit has regard or respect for the things of God.

## PRAISE WORSHIP

## PRAYER WARFARE

1. I decree that the programme of anti-Christ for my life will not prosper, in the name of Jesus.
2. Every power of anti-Christ in my life, die, in Jesus' name.
3. Glory of God, overshadow my life, in the name of Jesus.
4. Anti-Christ power, be disgraced, in the name of Jesus.
5. . Let the strongman known as the anti-Christ be rendered impotent, in the name of Jesus.
6. Let the voice of anti-Christ be silenced over my affairs, in the name

of Jesus.

7. I release myself from every grip of the anti-Christ, in the name of Jesus.

8. Every power, sponsoring anti-Christ programme in my destiny, dry up and die, in the name of Jesus.

9. I reverse every damage done to my life by the anti-Christ power, in the name of Jesus.

10. The deception of the anti-Christ will not function in my life, in the name of Jesus.

11. Glory of God, fill me with Your presence, in Jesus' name.

12. My Father, pull down every stronghold of the anti-Christ, in the name of Jesus.

13. Anti-Christ agenda for my salvation, be destroyed, in Jesus' name.

14. I bind every spirit of anti-Christ working against my spiritual growth, in the name of Jesus.

15. I shall not be a spiritual drop-out, in the name of Jesus.

16. I pull down every stronghold of the anti-Christ in my life, in the name of Jesus.

17. Thou power of God, swallow every deposit of the anti-Christ in my life, in the name of Jesus.

18. Every yoke of the anti-Christ, break, in the name of Jesus.

19. Every ladder through which the anti-Christ gains access to my life, be dismantled, in the name of Jesus.

20. I shall not be a slave to the anti-Christ, in the name of Jesus.

21. My Father, release me from every chain and fetter of the anti-Christ, in the name of Jesus.

22. I dethrone every kingdom of the anti-Christ in my life, in th name of Jesus.

# 47

# SPIRIT OF OPPRESSION

## INTRODUCTION

Acts 10:48 And he commanded them to be baptized in the name of the Lord. Then prayed they him to tarry certain days.

Oppressive spirits are tormenting spirits. They specialize in making life unbearable for their victims. The Bible says that oppression makes a wise man mad. Many victims of oppression battle with restlessness, sleeplessness, backwardness as well as physical and spiritual harassment.

## PRAISE WORSHIP

## PRAYER WARFARE

1. I pull down every stronghold of oppression in my life, in the name of Jesus.
2. I release myself from every yoke of the oppressor, in Jesus' name
3. Oppression must die in my life, in the name of Jesus.
4. Programme of oppression for my life, die, in Jesus' name.
5 Ancestral oppression, die, in the name of Jesus.

6. Every serpent and scorpion of oppression, I trample upon you, in the name of Jesus.
7. Dream of oppression, loose your hold, in the name of Jesus.
8. Witchcraft oppression, be neutralized, in Jesus' name.
9. Every strongman of oppression, die, in the name of Jesus.
10. I release my life from every yoke of oppression, in Jesus' name.
11. Power of oppression, die, in the name of Jesus.
12. I dismantle every dream of oppression, in the name of Jesus.
13. Holy Ghost fire, burn away every deposit of oppression, in the name of Jesus.
14. Spirit of oppression, loose your hold upon my life, in Jesus' name.
15. Let the oppressional capacity of my environment be neutralized, in the name of Jesus.
16. Every ladder of day and night oppression, break, in Jesus' name.
17. Every circle of oppression, break, in the name of Jesus.
18, I remove my destiny from familiar spirit oppression, in the name of Jesus.
19, Thou power of oppression of the night, die, in Jesus' name
20. Fire of God and thunder power of God, destroy and melt away every chain of oppression, in the name of Jesus.
21. Every power that is pressing me down, be dismantled, in the name of Jesus.

## INTRODUCTION

**Romans 8:15:** For ye have not received the spirit of bondage again to fear; but ye have received the Spirit of adoption, whereby we cry, Abba, Father.

This is a spirit of slavery and spiritual imprisonment. To be in bondage, is to be caged by habits, forces, inherited patterns, etc. When you are unable to arrest an evil habit in your life, you are in bondage.

# 48

# SPIRIT OF BONDAGE

## PRAISE WORSHIP

## PRAYER WARFARE

1. Ancestral bondage, break by the power in the blood of Jesus.
2. Territorial bondage, break by the power in the blood of Jesus.
3. Witchcraft bondage, break by the power in the blood of Jesus.
4. Familiar spirit bondage, break by the power in the blood of Jesus.
5. Infirmity bondage, break by the power in the blood of Jesus.
6. Dream bondage, break by the power in the blood of Jesus.
7. Emotional bondage, break by the power in the blood of Jesus.
8. Mental bondage, break by the power in the blood of Jesus.
9. Financial bondage, break by the power in the blood of Jesus.

10 Spiritual bondage, break by the power in the blood of Jesus.

11 Unconscious bondage, break by the power in the blood of Jesus.

12. Fire of God, destroy the ladder of bondage by the blood of Jesus.

13. Bondage of sorrow, break by the blood of Jesus.

14. Every power introducing bondage into my life, I pull you down, in the name of Jesus.

15. Every stronghold pressing me down, be dismantled, in Jesus' name.

16. I arrest every bondage supervisor, in the name of Jesus.

17. O God, arise and damage my bondage today, in Jesus' name.

18. Fire of God, arise with all your weapons of war and dismantle the strongman behind my bondage, in Jesus' name

19. Every progress arrester, be arrested, in Jesus' name.

20. Power of the oppressor, be disgraced, in the name of Jesus.

21. My life, rebel against every bondage, in the name of Jesus.

22. Every bondage of the power of the night, be broken, in the name of Jesus.

## INTRODUCTION

This is a spirit that antagonizes comfort and happiness; a spirit of deep anguish and melancholy.

# 49

# SORROWFUL SPIRIT

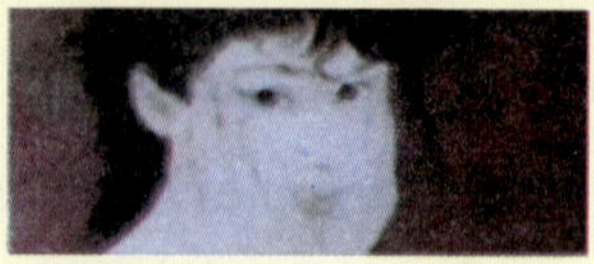

### PRAISE WORSHIP

### PRAYER WARFARE

1. I disband sorrow from my life, in the name of Jesus.
2. I evacuate the power of sadness from my spirit man, in the name of Jesus.
3. Yoke of sorrow, break, in the name of Jesus.
4. Spirit of melancholy, I break your stronghold, in Jesus' name.
5. Power of sorrow, die, in the name of Jesus.
6. I arrest every spirit of depression, in the name of Jesus.
7. Any power, warring against my emotional and mental health, be destroyed, in the name of Jesus.
8. I run into the divine tower of refuge, in the name of Jesus.
9. My life, reject sorrow, in the name of Jesus.
10. My family, reject sorrow, in the name of Jesus.
11. Thou power of tragedy, loose your hold, in the name of Jesus.
12. I reject the spirit of sorrow and sadness, in Jesus' name.
13. Let every power of heaviness shift away from my spirit, in the

name of Jesus.

14. I pull down every stronghold of sorrow, in the name of Jesus.
15. My Father, release me from every shackle of sorrow, in the name of Jesus.
16. My heart, reject the arrow of sorrow, in the name of Jesus.
17. I release myself from every yoke of sorrow, in Jesus' name.
18. Let my spirit man pick up the joy of the Lord, in Jesus' name.
19. I shall not eat the bread of sorrow, in the name of Jesus.
20. Let the power of God incubate my soul, in Jesus' name.
21. Let the joy of the Lord be my strength, in Jesus' name

# 50

# SPIRIT OF FEAR

## INTRODUCTION

**2 Tim. 1:7:** For God hath not given us the spirit of fear: but of power, and of love, and of a sound mind.

Fear has been described as the commonest demon in the world. It is a potent weapon used by the enemy to paralyse your faith. Fear enlarges the enemy's capacity. This spirit opens the gate for other destructive spirits.

## PRAISE WORSHIP

## PRAYER WARFARE

1. I bind and paralyse every strongman of fear in my life, in the mighty name of Jesus.
2. I loose myself from the bondage of fear, in Jesus' name.
3. I loose myself from all negative religious fears, bondage to traditions of demons and men, religious images and witchcraft prophets, in Jesus' name.
4. I loose myself from all demonic fears and from all their tormenting and enslaving powers, in Jesus' name.
5. I loose myself from every unholy fear of man, and I receive holy boldness, faith, confidence and inner strength, in Jesus' name.

6 Let all the entrances of fear into my life be closed forever, in the name of Jesus,

7 I plead the blood of Jesus over my heart, soul, spirit and body.

8. Let all the habitation of fear in my life be demolished, in Jesus name.

9. I bind every spirit of fear afflicting my life, in Jesus' name

10. I render you spirit of fear of ... (name them) powerless, in the name of Jesus.

11. I expel every spirit of fear in my life, in the name of Jesus.

12. O Lord, break the bands of fear in my life.

13. Let all fears emanating from parental influence, past association and guilt, depart from my spirit, in Jesus' name.

14. I command the strongholds of fear to break, in Jesus' name.

15. You spirit of fear, I command you to come out of your hiding places; depart from my mind, my emotions, my will, my spirit and my body, in the name of Jesus.

16. Let all the problems introduced by fear into my life depart now, in the name of Jesus.

17. I stand against the spirit of fear of:

- air planes - ambulances - failure - barbers
- other people's opinion - future - heights -flying
- cats - chicken - people - spiders
- Cancer - heart disease - dogs - water
- demons - insects - marriage - women
- robbers - Worms - blood - sleep

- skin diseases
- pregnancy
- children
- rivers
- fire
- death
- childbirth
- sexual Intercourse
- ridicule
- insanity
- poverty
- satan
- poison
- number 13
- mice
- disease
- dreams
- speed
- animals
- corpses
- crowds
-ghosts
- being alone
- being stared at
- darkness

,in the name of Jesus.

# 51

# SPIRIT OF INSANITY

## INTRODUCTION

**Luke 8:27:** And when he went forth to land, there met in out of the city a certain man, which had devils long time, and ware no clothes, neither abode in any house, but in the tombs.

This is the spirit that attacks the brain causing mental illness. Practically most cases of stubborn mental disorders, are arrows of darkness, aimed at turning lives upside down.

**PRAISES WORSHIP**

**Sing this song - There is power mighty in the Blood.**

**CONFESSIONS:**

**Psalm 25:16:** Turn thee unto me, and have mercy upon me: for I am desolete and afflicted.

**Psalm 25: 17:** The troubles of my heart are enlarged: O bring thou me out df my distresses.

**Psalm 25:20:** O keep my soul, and deliver me: let me not be ashamed: for I put my trust in thee.

**Psalm 9:9:** The Lord also will be a refuge for the oppressed, a refuge in times of trouble.

**Isa. 50:7:** For the Lord God will help me: therefore shall I not be confounded: therefore have I set my face like a flint and I know that I shall not be ashamed.

**2Cor. 19:5b:** . . . .bringing into captivity every thought to the obedience of Christ.

**Phil. 4:7:** And the peace of God, which passeth all understanding, shall keep your HEARTS and MINDS through Christ Jesus.

**2Tim. 1:7:** For God hath not given us the spirit of fear: but of power, and of love, and of a sound mind.

## PRAYER WARFARE

1. Father, I confess that in the past I had been unforgiving. I harboured bitterness and resentment in my heart, against certain people who had hurt or disappointed me.

2. I now recognise this as a sin, and confess it as sin, for You have said in Your word, that if we confess our sins, You are faithful and just to forgive us our sins and to cleanse us of all unrighteousness (1 John 1:9).

3. I now forgive the following people, that I can remember, who had hurt or disappointed me. (Mention names of those who come to your mind.) I now freely forgive all these people and ask You to bless them if they are still living. I also forgive myself for all my faults and failures, for You have freely forgiven me.

4. Thank You Father for freedom from the load of unforgiveness, bitterness and resentment, in Jesus' name.

5. Father, I confess to You, that in the past, through ignorance, curiosity or wilfulness, I came in contact with certain sinful acts. I now recognise them as sin and confess them as sin, and ask for forgiveness, in Jesus' name.

6. I also renounce and confess as sin, any oath which I have made to any false god and any idolatry, in which I have been involved.

7 Satan, I rebuke you, in the name of Jesus, I close any door, which I or my ancestors may have opened to you and your demons, in the name of Jesus.

8. I renounce satan and all his demons; I declare them my enemies, and command them to come out of my life completely, in the name of Jesus.

9. In the name of Jesus Christ, I now claim deliverance from all evil spirits which may be in me (Joel 2:28). Once and for all, I close the door in my life to all occult practices and command all related spirits to leave me now, in Jesus' name.

10. I break every curse of mental destruction, in Jesus' name.

11. I release myself from the hold of any evil strongman, in the name of Jesus.

12. I command all spirits of confusion to loose their hold upon my life, in the name of Jesus.

13. Call the spirits you do not desire in your life by name. Then issue the command firmly and repeatedly that they must come out, in the name of the Lord Jesus.

14. Pray as follows: You spirit of

| | | |
|---|---|---|
| - mental illness | - hallucination | - insanity |
| - lunacy | - neurosis | -anxiety |
| - depression | - hysteria | - compulsive behaviours |
| - personality disorder | | - sexual deviation |
| - alcoholism | | - premature ageing |

- double-mindedness
- retardation
- convulsion
- vandalism
- murder
- destruction
- rage
- mind darkness
- incoherence
- mind dullness
- apathy
- day dreaming
- inactivity
- indifference
- sloth
- stupidity
- trance
- unreasonable behaviours
- addiction and bondage to drugs of:

marijuana, LSD (acid), cocaine, heroin, valium, amphetamines, barbiturates, tranquilizers, aspirin, caffeine, nicotine, come out of my brain and mind, in the name of Jesus.

15. I loose myself from you, in the name of Jesus, and I command you to leave me right now, in the mighty name of our Lord Jesus Christ.

# 52

# SPIRIT OF HEAVINESS

## INTRODUCTION

**Isaiah 61;3:** To appoint unto them that mourn in Zion, to give unto them beauty for ashes, the oil of joy for mourning, the garment of praise for the spirit of heaviness; that they might be called trees of righteousness, the planting of the Lord, that he might be glorified.

Spirit of heaviness is a dark shadow and burden which envelopes the soul and Swallows happiness. Those under the attack of this spirit feel depressed, low, weak, faint, confused and hopeless.

**PRAISE WORSHIP**

**PRAYER WARFARE**

1. The dark shadow of the soul, clear away by the blood of Jesus.
2. Power of heavy heart, loose your hold upon my life, in Jesus' name.
3 .Power of heaviness, be dismantled from my soul, in Jesus' name.
4. Let the garment of praise replace the spirit of heaviness, in the name of Jesus.
5. Holy Ghost fire, melt away every darkness of heaviness in my

soul, in the name of Jesus.

6. I release myself from the case of discouragement, in Jesus' name.
7. Power of God, move my life from strength to strength and from glory to glory, in the name of Jesus.
8. I reject every oppressive spirit hanging on my soul, in Jesus' name.
9. There shall be no more heaviness for my soul, in Jesus' name.
10. Let the spirit of heaviness loose its hold upon my spirit man, in the name of Jesus.
11. I bind every power of depression and cast it out, in Jesus' name.
12. Fire of God, burn to ashes every garment of heaviness, in the name of Jesus.
13. I pull down the masquerading powers working against my happiness, in the name of Jesus.
14. Every power militating against my joy, die, in Jesus' name.
15. I bind and cast out every enemy of my full-scale laughter, in the name of Jesus.
16. I rise above every hand pointing at my joy, in Jesus'
17. Every spider of darkness enclosing my heart, clear away, in the name of Jesus.
18. I dismantle every rope of darkness arresting my freedom, in the name of Jesus.
19. Every power that has been stealing from me, loose your power, in the name of Jesus.
20. I bury forever every yoke of heaviness, in the name of Jesus.

21 I drink from the well of salvation, in the name of Jesus.

22. I shall not become a slave to the power of heaviness, in the name of Jesus.

23. Every power working against my mental health, be dismantled, in the name of Jesus.

24. Every burden of darkness enclosing my soul, clear away, in the name of Jesus.

# 53

# SPIRIT OF INJURY

## INTRODUCTION

**Mark 9:22:** And ofttimes it hath cast him into the fire, and into the waters, to destroy him: but if thou canst do any thing, have compassion on us, and help us.

This is a spirit that sponsors self-destruction and self-hurt. Its victims will be prone to injury, accidents and unexplainable disaster.

## PRAISE WORSHIP

## PRAYER WARFARE

1. Thou power of self-destruction, be dismantled, in Jesus' name.
2. I release my life from every internal oppression, in Jesus' name.
3. Every mantle of injury, be dismantled, in Jesus' name.
4. O God, arise and let every oppressive spirit be buried, in the name of Jesus.
5. Every proneness to injury, be destroyed, in Jesus' name.
6. Power of self-injury, die, in the name of Jesus.
7. Every handwriting of arrows of affliction, be wiped off by the blood of Jesus.
8. Holy Ghost fire, burn to ashes every plantation of destruction in

my life, in the name of Jesus.

9. I take divine insurance against every threat of accident and injury, in the name of Jesus.

10 I shall not die but live to declare the works of God, in Jesus' name.

11. I bind and cast out every arrow of the terminators, in Jesus' name.

12. Glory of God, overshadow my life, in the name of Jesus.

13. I arise by the power of God to overcome every dart of the oppressor, in the name of Jesus.

14. I pull down every stronghold of the oppressor, in Jesus' name.

15. Every strongman attached to my health, be destroyed, in the name of Jesus.

16. My life is not for sale, in the name of Jesus.

17. Every serpent and scorpion of self-harm, I trample upon you, in the name of Jesus.

18. Every power monitoring my health for evil, fall down and die, in the name of Jesus.

19, Power of long life, come upon me from the bosom of God, in the name of Jesus.

20. I fire back every arrow of internal evil command, in Jesus' name.

21. Fire of God's judgement, arise and destroy every evil imagination targeted at me, in the name of Jesus.

22, I shall not destroy my body, soul and spirit, in Jesus' name.

# 54

# SPIRIT OF WHOREDOM

## INTRODUCTION

**Hosea 4:12:** My people ask counsel at their stocks, and heir staff declareth unto them: for the spirit of whoredoms hath caused them to err, and they have gone a whoring from under their God.

This spirit is responsible for all manner of sexual perversions. It controls homo-sexuality, prostitution, fornication, lesbianism, oral sex, anal sex, incest, etc. Venereal diseases, flirting and seductive body movements are all manifestations of this spirit.

**PRAISE WORSHIP**

**PRAYER WARFARE**

1. Thank God for His power to deliver from every bondage.
2. I break myself loose from every spirit of sexual perversion, in the name of Jesus.
3. I release myself from every spiritual pollution emanating from my past sins of fornication and sexual immorality, in Jesus' name
4. I release myself from every ancestral pollution, in Jesus' name.
5. I release myself from every dream pollution, in Jesus' name
6. I command every evil plantation of sexual perversion in my life, to

come out with all its roots, in the name of Jesus.

7 Every spirit of sexual perversion working against my life, be paralyzed and get out of my life, in the name of Jesus.

8 Every demon of sexual perversion, assigned against my life, be bound in the name of Jesus.

9 Father Lord, let the power of sexual perversion oppressing my life receive the fire of God and be roasted, in the name of Jesus.

10. Every inherited demon of sexual perversion in my life, receive the arrows of fire and remain permanently bound, in Jesus' name.

11. I command every force of the power of sexual perversion to come against themselves, in the name of Jesus.

12. Father Lord, let every demonic stronghold built in my life by the spirit of sexual perversion, be pulled down, in Jesus' name.

13. Let every power of sexual perversion, that has summoned my life be shattered to pieces, in the name of Jesus.

14, Let my soul be delivered from the forces of sexual perversion, in the name of Jesus.

15. Let the Lord God of Elijah arise, with a strong hand against every spirit husband/wife and power of sexual perversion, in Jesus' name.

16. I break the hold of any evil power over my life, in Jesus' name.

17. I nullify every effect of the bite of sexual perversion, upon my life, in the name of Jesus.

18, Every evil stranger and satanic deposit in my life, I command you to be paralyzed and get out of my life, in Jesus' name.

19. Holy Ghost Fire, purge my life completely, in Jesus' name.

20. I claim complete deliverance from the spirit of fornication and sexual immorality, in Jesus' name.
21. Let my eyes be delivered from lustfulness, in Jesus' name.
22. As from today, let my eyes be controlled by the Holy Spirit, in the name of Jesus.
23. Holy Ghost Fire, fall upon my eyes and burn to ashes every evil force and satanic power, controlling them, in Jesus' name.
24. I move from bondage to liberty in every area of my life, in the name off Jesus.
25. Thank God for answers to your prayers.

# 55

## HAUGHTY SPIRIT

Pride

### INTRODUCTION

**Proverbs 16:1819:** Pride goeth before destruction, and an haughty spirit before a fal. " Better it is to be of an humble spirit with the lowly, than to divide the spoil with the proud. Pride is probably the first sin in the universe. Lucifer lifted himself against God. Pride is over-evaluation of oneself and accomplishments. To be possessed by this spirit is to be in the school of physical and spiritual destruction.

**PRAISE WORSHIP**

**PRAYER WARFARE**

1. I repent of every sin of pride, in the name of Jesus.
2. I bind and cast out every snobbish spirit, in Jesus' name.
3. I barricade my life from every arrow of self-importance, in the name of Jesus.
4. I release myself from every unteachable spirit, in Jesus' name.
5. I shall not be a student in the school of rebellion, in Jesus' name.
6. Every inherited power of pride, die, in the name of Jesus.
7. Shall not rebel against divinely ordained pastoral authority, in

the name of Jesus.

8. Thou negative power of stiff-neck and obstinacy, die, in the name of Jesus.

9. I dismantle every stronghold of "braggadocios", in Jesus' name.

10. I pull down every citadel of boastfulness, in Jesus' name.

11. I repent from every better-than-thou-attitude, in Jesus' name.

12. I shall not reject any divine order, in the name of Jesus.

13. Every spirit of gossip and envy, come out with all your roots, ir the name of Jesus.

14. Every power, delegated to destroy my destiny, die, in Jesus name.

15. Holy Ghost fire, melt away every power of self-praise in my life in the name of Jesus.

16. Every power of idleness and confusion, loose your hold, in th name of Jesus.

17. I shall not be a student in any Luciferin school, in Jesus' name.

18. Let the power of humility come upon my spirit, in Jesus' nane

19. I shall not dig my own grave with my mouth, in Jesus' name.

20. Holy fire from the altar of God, burn away every deception in m life, in the name of Jesus.

21. Every yoke of destruction, be destroyed, in Jesus' name.

22. Holy Ghost fire, flush out every plantation of darkness in my sot in the name of Jesus.

23. Everything that pride has stolen in my life, be restored, in t name of Jesus.

# 56

# LYING SPIRIT

## INTRODUCTION

1 Kings 22:21-23 And there came forth a spirit, and stood before the Lord, and said, I will persuade him. And the Lord said unto him, Wherewith? And he said, I will go forth, and I will be a lying spirit in the mouth of all his prophets. And he said, Thou shalt persuade him, and prevail also: go forth, and do so. 23 Now therefore, behold, the Lord hath put a lying spirit in the mouth of all these thy prophets, and the Lord hath spoken evil concerning thee.

This is the spirit that hates the truth and sets out to propagate and establish lies. All compulsive liars are under the control of this spirit of death and hell.

## PRAISE WORSHIP

## PRAYER WARFARE

1. I repent from every falsehood, in the name of Jesus.
2. Blood of Jesus, wipe away every sin of lying, in Jesus' name.
3. I refuse to be fathered by the father of lies, who is satan, in the name of Jesus.

4. I release myself from every curse of following lies, in Jesus name.
5. I release myself from every inherited lying spirit, in Jesus' name.
6. I receive deliverance from every delusive behaviour, in the name of Jesus.
7. I bind and cast out every spirit of hypocrisy, in Jesus' name.
8. O God, arise and let all the enemies of truth in my life scatter in the name of Jesus.
9. Every power of falsehood in my life, die, in Jesus' name.
10, I repent from every sin of talkativeness and qossip, in Jesus' name.
11. Thou spirit of exaggeration, get out of my life, in Jesus' name.
12. I receive deliverance from every sin of flattery, in Jesus' name.
13. I refuse to believe and follow a lie, in Jesus' name.
14 Every lying spirit, present in my dream life, be buried, in the name of Jesus.
15. I shall not become a victim of demonic manipulation, in Jesus' name.
16. Every power of deception and profanity, depart from my life, in the name of Jesus.
17. I receive deliverance from the power of lying spirits, in the name of Jesus.
18. My life, receive the touch of heaven, in the name of Jesus.
19. My tongue, receive deliverance by fire, in the name of Jesus.
20. Holy Spirit, incubate my soul with Your truth, in Jesus' name.

21. Thou Way, Truth and Life, overshadow my life, in Jesus' name.
22. My spirit-man, receive the fire of God, in the name of Jesus.
23. Every problem brought into my life by lying spirits, be dismantled, in the name of Jesus.
24. Every yoke of instability, break, in the name of Jesus.

# 57

# UNCLEAN SPIRIT

## INTRODUCTION

**Mark 5:8:** For he said unto him, Come out of the man, thou unclean spirit.

This is the spirit responsible for dirty physical and spiritual lives. It manifests in polluted thoughts, destructive dirty habits and environmental pollution that cause general defilement of the spirit man. It is a wicked spirit that can violate one's spirit.

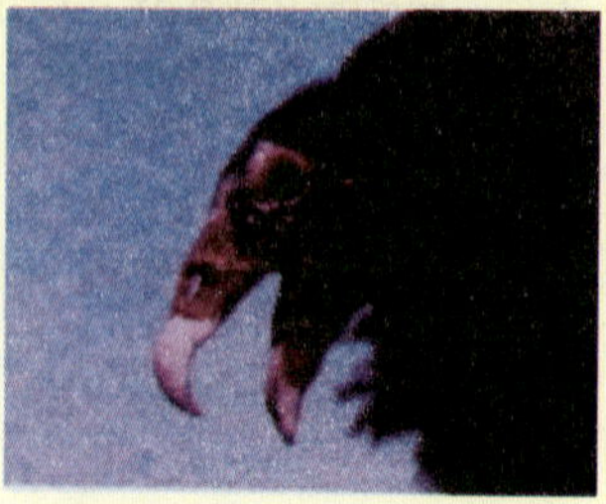

## PRAISE WORSHIP

## PRAYER WARFARE

1. Every conspiracy targeted at my life in the heavenlies, scatter, in the name of Jesus.
2. I release myself from every generational bondage, in Jesus' name.
3. I break the stronghold of every power of wickedness targeted at me, in the name of Jesus.
4. Blood of Jesus, wipe off every spiritual defilement from my life, in the name of Jesus.
5. Every dark spirit, loose your hold, in the name of Jesus.
6. Every door opened to dark powers, be closed, in Jesus' name.
7. Every attack against my spirit-man, be frustrated, in Jesus' name.
8. O God, arise and let every unclean spirit scatter, in Jesus' name.

9. I shall not be a victim of demonic oppression, in Jesus' name.
10. Holy Ghost fire, burn away all spiritual rags, in Jesus' name.
11. I bind and cast out every power of sleep and dream disturbance, in the name of Jesus.
12. Every self-destructive power, die, in the name of Jesus.
13. Any demonically sponsored gift or talent, die, in Jesus' name.
14. Every power of the grave, loose your hold, in Jesus' name.
15. Every inner torment and conflict, cease, in Jesus' name.
16. Every senseless behaviour, release my life, in Jesus' name.
17. Every power behind nightmares, be dismantled, in Jesus' name.
18. I shall not hear strange voices, in the name of Jesus.
19. I release myself from every power of sexual perversion, in the name of Jesus.
20. Every power controlling my life negatively, die, in Jesus' name
21. Every dream attack, be dismantled, in the name of Jesus.
22. O God of Elijah, arise in Your fire and power and pursue my pursuers, in the name of Jesus.
23. I expel from my life any spirit which is not of God, in Jesus' name.
24. My life, reject all satanic flying arrows, in the name of Jesus.
25. Every unprofitable fascination, be dismantled, in Jesus' name.
26. Sword of the Lord's deliverance, deliver me by fire, in Jesus' name.
27. Every door opened to unclean spirits, be closed, in Jesus' name.
28. Blood of Jesus, arise with Your weapons of war and cause mighty deliverance in my life, in the name of Jesus.

29. O God, make me a walking advertisement of Your power, in the name of Jesus.

30. I receive deliverance from every satanic embargo, in Jesus' name.

# 58

# DEAF AND DUMB SPIRIT

## INTRODUCTION

**Mark 9:17-27:** And one of the multitude answered and said, Master, I have brought unto thee my son, which hath a dumb spirit: And wheresoever he taketh him, he teareth him: and he foameth, and gnasheth with his teeth, and pineth away: and I spake to thy disciples that they should cast him out: and they could not. He answereth him, and saith, O faithless generation, how long shall I be with you? how long shall I suffer you? bring him unto me. And they brought him unto him: and when he saw him, straightway the spirit tare him; and he fell on the ground, and wallowed foaming. And he asked his father, How long is it ago since this came unto him? And he said, of a child. And ofttimes it hath cast him into the fire, and into the waters, to destroy him: but if thou canst do any thing, have compassion on us, and help us. Jesus said unto him, If thou canst believe, all things are possible to him that believeth. And straightway the father of the child cried out, and said with tears, Lord, I believe; help thou mine unbelief. When Jesus saw that the people came running together,

## DEAF AND DUMB SPIRIT contd

he rebuked the foul spirit, saying unto him, Thou dumb and deaf spirit, I charge thee, come out of him, and enter no more into him. And the spirit cried, and rent him sore, and came out of him: and he was as one dead; insomuch that many said, He is dead. But Jesus took him by the hand, and lifted him up: and he arose.

These are spirits that affects the ability to hear and speak. It may manifest stammering or partial deafness. We need to know that it is a destiny destroying spirit.

### PRAISE WORSHIP

### PRAYER WARFARE

1. Father, destroy every handwriting of wickedness, in Jesus' name.
2. I bind and cast out every spirit of deafness and dumbness, in the name of Jesus.
3. Every evil effect of early childhood trauma in my life, be dismantled, in the name of Jesus.
4. Power of God, speak "ephatha", to my spiritual ears, in Jesus name
5. Let the dumbness and the deafness of the spirit melt away, in the name of Jesus.

6. Father in the name of Jesus, pull down every citadel of the deaf and dumb spirit in my life.
7. I bind and cast out every deaf and dumb spirit, in Jesus' name.
8. Every self-punishing power working against me, die, in Jesus' name.
9. I release myself from the bondage of any ear problems, in the name of Jesus.
10. Every inherited deaf and dumb spirit, loose your hold, in the name of Jesus.
11. I shall arise and overcome every arrow of infirmity, fired into my brain, in the name of Jesus.
12. O God arise, and let every yoke of affliction scatter.
13. Blood of Jesus, flow into every organ of my body and make me whole, in the name of Jesus.
14. Every inherited oppression, be dismantled, in Jesus' name.
15. I cut off from my destiny any arrow fired into my mouth or ear faculty, in the name of Jesus.
16. Holy Ghost fire, burn to ashes every plantation of speech and hearing impairment, in the name of Jesus.
17. Every power magnetizing retrogression into my progress, die, in the name of Jesus.
18. Glory of God, overshadow my life, in the name of Jesus.
19. Every power working against my progress, I bind and cast you out,in the name of Jesus.
20. I shall not be a victim of speech and hearing manipulators, in The name of Jesus.

21. Spirit of the living God, overshadow my faculties, in Jesus' name.
22. Let the resurrection power of Jesus fall upon my faculties, in the name of Jesus.
23. Any virtue stolen from my life by the powers of darkness, be released, in the name of Jesus.
24. I bind and cast out every activity of the amputator, in the name of Jesus.
25. Every arrow fired against my speech and hearing faculties in the dream, go back to the sender, in the name of Jesus.
26. O Lord, save me and I shall be saved; heal me and I shall be healed, in the name of Jesus.
27. Thou power of deafness and dumbness, die, in Jesus' name.

# 59

# SPIRIT OF THE WORLD

## INTRODUCTION

**1 Cor. 2;12:** Now we have received, not the spirit of the world, but the spirit which is of God; that we might know the things that are freely given to us of God.

This is the spirit that makes people carnal and ungodly. It drawS men and women to worldliness, godlessness, pleasure and entertainment while completely forgetting God. Compromise and hanging out with the wrong crowd is the order of the day in the life of its victims.

## PRAISE WORSHIP

## CONFESSIONS

**Galatians g:13-14:** Christ hath redeemed us from the curse of the law, beirng made a curse for us: for it is written, Cursed is every one that hangeth on a tree: That the blessing of Abraham might come on the Gentiles through Jesus Christ: that we might receive the promise of the Spirit through faith.

**1 Tim 4:18:** And the Lord shall deliver me from every evil work, and Will preserve me unto his heavenly kingdom: to whom be glory for ever and ever. Amen.

**Col. 1:13:** Who hath delivered us from the power of darkness, and hath translated us into the kingdom of his dear Son:

**Col. 2:15:** And having spoiled principalities and powers, he made a shew of Them openly, triumphing over them in it.

## PRAYER WARFARE

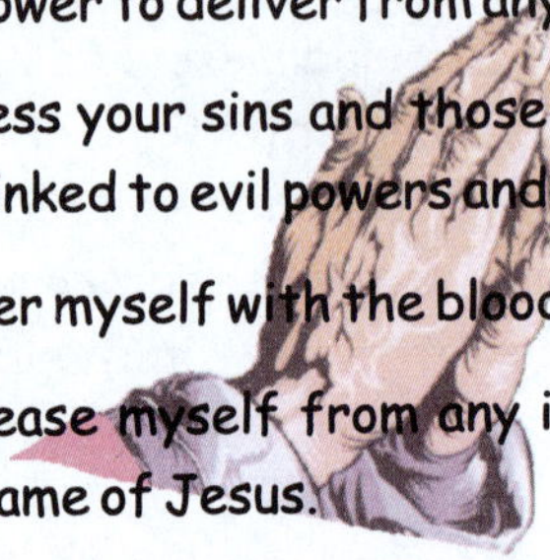

1. Thank God for HIS mighty power to save to the uttermost and for power to deliver from any form of bondage.
2. Confess your sins and those of your ancestors, especially those sins linked to evil powers and idolatry.
3. I cover myself with the blood of Jesus.
4. I release myself from any inherited bondage and limitation, in the name of Jesus.
5. O Lord, send Your axe of fire to the foundation of my life and destroy every evil plantation.
6. Let the blood of Jesus flush out from my system every inherited satanic deposit, in the name of Jesus.
7. I release myself from the grip of any problem transferred into my life from the womb, in the name of Jesus.
8. Let the blood of Jesus and the fire of the Holy Ghost cleanse every organ in my body, in the name of Jesus.
9. I break and loose myself from every inherited evil covenant, in the name of Jesus.
10. I break and loose myself from every inherited evil curse, in the name of Jesus.
11. I vomit every evil consumption that I have been fed with as a child, in the name of Jesus.

12. I command all foundational strongmen attached to my life to be paralysed, in the name of Jesus.

13. Let any rod of the wicked rising against my family line be rendered impotent for my sake, in the name of Jesus.

14. I cancel the consequences of any evil local name attached to my person, in the name of Jesus.

15. Pray aggressively against the following evil foundations. Pray as follows: You (pick the under-listed one by one), loose your hold over my life and be purged out of my foundation, in Jesus' name.
destructive effect of polygamy - evil physical design
- unscriptural manners of conception - parental curses
- envious rivalry - demonic blood transfusion
- evil dedication - demonic alteration of destiny
- demonic incisions - demonic marriage
- dream pollution - evil laying on of hands
- demonic sacrifice - fellowship with family idols
- fellowship with local idols
- fellowship with demonic consultants
- wrong exposure to sex - exposure to evil diviner
- demonic initiations - inherited infirmity

16. You evil foundational plantations, come out of my life with all your roots, in the name of Jesus.

17. I break and loose myself from every form of demonic bewitchment, in the name of Jesus.

18. I release myself from every evil domination and control, in the

name of Jesus.

19. Let the blood of Jesus be transfused into my blood vessel.

20 Let every gate opened to the enemy by my foundation be closed forever with the blood of Jesus.

21. Lord Jesus, walk back into every second of my life and deliver me where I need deliverance, heal me where I need healing. transform me where I need transformation.

22. Let the power in the blood of Jesus separate me from the sins of my ancestors.

23. Let the blood of Jesus remove any unprogressive label from every aspect of my life.

24. O Lord, create in me a clean heart by Your power.

25. O Lord, renew a right spirit within me.

26. O Lord, teach me to die to self.

27. O Lord, ignite my calling with Your fire.

28. O Lord, anoint me to pray without ceasing.

29. O Lord, establish me as a holy person unto You.

30. O Lord, restore my spiritual eyes and ears in Jesus' name.

31. O Lord, let the anointing to excel in my spiritual and physical life fall on me.

32. O Lord, produce in me the power of self-control and gentleness.

33. O Lord, let the anointing of the Holy Spirit break every yoke of backwardness in my life.

34. Holy Ghost, breathe on me now, in the name of Jesus.

35. Holy Ghost fire, ignite me to the glory of God.

36. Let every rebellion flee from my heart, in Jesus' name.
37. I command every spiritual contamination in my life to receive cleansing by the blood of Jesus.
38. Let the brush of the Lord scrub out every dirtiness in my spiritual pipe, in the name of Jesus.
39. Every rusted spiritual pipe in my life, receive wholeness, in the name of Jesus.
40. I command every power eating up my spiritual pipe to be roasted, in the name of Jesus.
41. I renounce any evil dedication placed upon my life, in Jesus' name.
42. I break every evil edict and ordination, in Jesus' name
43. O Lord, cleanse all the soiled parts of my life.
44. O Lord, deliver me from every foundational pharaoh.
45. O Lord, heal every wounded part of my life.
46. O Lord, bend every evil rigidity in my life.
47 O Lord, re-align every satanic straying in my life.
48. O Lord, let the fire of the Holy Spirit warm every satanic freezing in my life.
49. O Lord, give me a life that kills death.
50. O Lord, kindle in me the fire of charity.
51. O Lord, glue me together where I am oppossed to myself.
52. O Lord, enrich me with Your gifts.
53. O Lord, quicken me and increase my desire of the things of heaven.
54. By Your rulership. O Lord, let the lust of the flesh in my life die

55. Lord Jesus, increase daily in my life.

56. Lord Jesus, maintain Your gifts in my life.

57. O Lord, refine and purge my life by Your fire.

58. Holy Spirit, inflame and fire my heart, in Jesus' name.

59, Holy Ghost fire, begin to burn away every power of the bond woman in me, in the name of Jesus.

60. O Lord, make me ready to go wherever You send me.

61. Lord Jesus, never let me shut You out.

62 Lord Jesus, work freely in me and through me.

# 60

# SPIRIT OF TREACHERY

## INTRODUCTION

**Judges 9:23:** Then God sent an evil spirit between Abimeteh and the men of Shechem and the men of Shechem dealt treacherously with Abimelech: This is the spirit responsible for disloyalty, treason, unreliability, deceit and betrayal of trust. It has caused the breaking up of churches into factions etc.

## PRAISE WORSHIP

## PRAYER WARFARE

1 I refuse to be manipulated into rebellion, in Jesus name

2. I bind and cast out every spirit of treachery, in Jesus name.

3 Every conspiracy fashioned against me scatter, in Jesus name.

4. Every conspiracy in the heavenlies against my life, scatter, in the name of Jesus

5. Let every spirit of contention fashioned against me, scatter, in the name of Jesus

6 I restrain every raging spirit from harassing my destiny, in the name of Jesus.

7. Every spirit of treachery and disloyalty, be disgraced, in the

name of Jesus.

8. Thou power of God move into the midst of the camp of disloyalty and cause a scattering, in the name of Jesus

9. Every evil programne designed against my breakthrough, be dismantled, in the name of Jesus

10. I purge myself from every evil deposit and satanic influence, in the name of Jesus.

11. Let the yoke of satanic programmers break to pieces, in the name of Jesus.

12. I destroy the pattern of evil that has monitored my life, in the name of Jesus.

13. I shall not swallow the hook of the enemy, in Jesus' name.

14. I destroy every programme of darkness fashioned against my life in the name of Jesus.

15. I command my life to break from the yoke of the oppressor, in the name of Jesus.

# 61

# SPIRIT OF MURDER

## INTRODUCTION

This spirit is blood thirsty and kills without mercy. It does not value human life. It is responsible for wars.

## PRAISE WORSHIP

## PRAYER WARFARE

1. I release myself from every spirit of hatred, in Jesus' name.
2. Angels of the living God, encamp around me, in Jesus name.
3. Any dark power that wants me to die, die, in Jesus' name.
4. Thou power that kills without hands, loose your hold, in the name of Jesus,
5. Every power of family destruction, die, in Jesus name.
6. Every power of health destruction, die, in Jesus' name.
7. I refuse to be a victim of untimely death, in Jesus name.
8. I rise above every threat of elimination, in Jesus' name.
9. Any power hired to curse me, fall after the order of Balaam, in the name of Jesus.

10. I shall not die but live to declare the works of God, in Jesus name.
11. I rise above every yoke of the oppressors, in Jesus name.
12. Power of murder, loose your grip, in the name of Jesus
13. Every blood-thirsty demon, loose your hold, in Jesus name.
14. Let the spirit of compassion overshadow my life, in Jesus name.
15. Let my life reject every case of murder, in Jesus name
16. Every attack of senseless violence against my life, melt away, in the name of Jesus.
17. Every spiritual and physical hired assassin, be neutralized, in the name of Jesus.
18. No weapon of death fashioned against me shall prosper, in the name of Jesus
19. My hand shall be on the neck of my oppressors, in Jesus name
20. Every blood-thirsty adversary, be disgraced, in Jesus name
21. Holy Ghost, arise with Your weapon of fire and pursue every blood-thirsty pursuer, in the name of Jesus
22. Let the weapons of death fashioned against my well-being be dismantled, in the name of Jesus.
23. Divine wall of fire, envelope me, in the name of Jesus
24. Divine shadow of God, envelope my life, in Jesus name.

# 62

# PERVERSE SPIRIT

## INTRODUCTION

**Isaiah 19:14:** The Lord hath mingled a perverse spirit in the midst thereof and they have caused Egypt to err in every work thereof, as a drunken man staggereth in hie vomit

This is o spirit that causes perversion distraction and confusion. It also makes people stray and make wrong decision. A consistent walk in error, is part of its manifestation.

## PRAISE WORSHIP

## PRAYER WARFARE

1. I repent from the sin of following satanic manipulation into my life. in the name of Jesus
2. I release myself from every generational curse bringing perversion into my life in the name of Jesus
3. Every power of Idolatry in my family line, be dismantled, in the name of Jesus
4. Every power of sexual perversion, loose your hold, in Jesus name.
5. I release myself from any form of addiction, in Jesus name.
6. I recover myself from the school of repeated disobedience to God, in the name of Jesus

7. Every hardness of heart, melt away by the fire of the Holy Ghost, in the name of Jesus.
8. Thou power of stubborness, die, in the name of Jesus.
9. Blood of Jesus, clean and wipe away every filthiness in my spirit-man, in the name of Jesus.
10 Every power polluting my mind be buried alive, in Jesus' name
11 Every spirit of error, loose your hold upon my life, in Jesus' name
12. I shall be a winner in every area of my life, in Jesus' name.
13. Holy Ghost fire, burn to ashes every handwriting of wickedness targeted at me, in the name of Jesus,
14. Let the fire of God barricade my mind from the fiery darts of the wicked, in the name of Jesus.
15 I refuse to tarry in the valley of confusion, in Jesus' name.
16. I bind and cast out every perversion of my hands, in Jesus' name
17 I bind and cast out every perversion of my head, in Jesus' name
18. I bind and cast out every perversion of my legs, in Jesus' name
19. I reject every night manipulation by satanic agents, in Jesus' name.
20. I expel from my life every spirit of manipulation, in Jesus' name
21. O God, arise and deliver me from every polluting spirit, in the name of Jesus.
22. I refuse to be a student in the school of perversion of the word of God and heresy, in the name of Jesus.
23. Every form of foolishness Targeted at my heart, melt away by the fire of the Holy Spirit, in Jesus' name.

24. Every conspiracy against my divine assignment, scatter, in the name of Jesus.

25. Holy Ghost fire, arise with Your weapons of war and set me free from every internal cage, in the name of Jesus.

## INTRODUCTION

**Palm 27:1-2:** The Lord is my light and
my salvation whom s hall I fear? the LORD
the strength of my life: of whom shall I be afraid?
2 When the wicked, even mine enemies
and my foes, came upon me to eat up my
flesh, they stumbled and fell.

**Isaiah 49:2-26** But thus saith the LORD, Even the batives of the mighty shall be taken away, and the prey of the terrible shall be delivered: for I will contend with him that contendeth with thee, and I will save thy children And I will feed them that oppress thee with their own flesh; and they shall be drunken with their own blood, as with sweet wine: and all flesh shall know that I the LORD am thy Saviour and thy Redeemer, the mighty One of Jacob.

These are destructive powers who see the human body as food and the blood as drink. Many people have fallen victim of these strange powers. Many have also died before their time, and many destinies have been Swallowed. A copy of our message on Eaters of Flesh and Drinkers of Blood would be very helpful.

# 63

# EATERS OF FLESH AND DRINKERS OF BLOOD

PRAISE WORSHIP

## PRAYER WARFARE

1. O God, be my light and salvation, in the name of Jesus
2. O God, be the strength of my life, in the name of Jesus
3. O God, I render my life safe by Your power, in Jesus name.
4. Let every power and activity of the eaters of flesh and drinkers of blood die, in the name of Jesus.
5. Eaters of flesh and drinkers of blood, drink your blood and eat your own flesh, in the name of Jesus.
6. I bind and cast out every power of the eaters of flesh and drinkers of blood, in the name of Jesus.
7. Let the eaters of flesh and drinkers of blood release my virtues, in the name of Jesus.
8. Let the captive of the mighty be released, in Jesus name.
9. Let the captive of the terrible be released, in Jesus name.
10. I declare freedom upon my life, in the name of Jesus.
11. Let the power of the blood-thirsty demons be dismantled, in the name of Jesus.
12 I remove my name from the book of eaters of flesh and drinkers of blood, in the name of Jesus.
13. I pull down the stronghold of the eaters of flesh and drinkers of blood, in the name of Jesus.
14. Fire of God, burn to ashes the agenda of the eaters of flesh and drinkers of blood, in the name of Jesus.
15. I break every covenant of destruction of my health, in Jesus name
16. Holy Ghost fire, enter into my blood stream and flush out all the

poison of darkness, in the name of Jesus,

17. My life, become too hot for witchcraft to handle, in Jesus name.

18. I bind and cast out any deposit of darkness in any part of my body, in the name of Jesus.

19, I receive power, to disgrace every blood-thirsty aggressor, in the name of Jesus,

20. Arrows of death, backfire, in the name of Jesus.

# 64
# COMPULSIVE EATING SPIRITS

## INTRODUCTION

These are spirits that have the tendency to make one eat and drink excessively resulting in serious health problems and eventually shorten the life of their victims

**PRAISE WORSHIP**

**PRAYER WARFARE**

1. I reject being a slave of food, in the name of Jesus.
2. My mouth gate will not destroy my life, in the name of Jesus
3. Let the power-ofiprayer and fasting fall upon my life, in the name of Jesus.
4 My body, reject every demonic food, in the name of Jesus.
5. Every arrow fired at my health through the mouth gate, back fine, in the name of Jesus.
6. Every gluttonous spirit, loose your hold, in the name of Jesus.
7. I shall not eat myself to death, in the name of Jesus.
8. Every1 poison that I have eaten or swallowed, be vomited, in the name of Jesus.

9. Demonic fatness, melt away, in the name of Jesus
10. Spiritual feeding, melt away in the name of Jesus
11 I overcome every addiction, in the name of Jesus.
12. Overeating demons, loose your hold upon my life, in Jesus name.
13. O Lord, let me have the power to arrest every demonic craving in Jesus name.
14. I shall not become a play thing in the hands of the spirit of gluttony, in the name of Jesus.
15 My life, reject every power of compulsive eating, in Jesus name
16. I arise above every power of compulsive eating, in Jesus name.
17. I reject every power working against the glory of God for my life, in the name of Jesus.
18. I shall trample upon every serpent and scorpion of gluttony, in the name of Jesus.
19. Holy Ghost fire, sanitize my system, in the name of Jesus.
20 The power of self-control, come upon my life, in Jesus name
21 Help me O Lord, to control my mouth, in the name of Jesus.

# 65

# SPIRITS OF FAILURE

## INTRODUCTION

These are anti-success spirits. They bring failure into situations that are targeted towards success. They introduce various kinds of failures into people's lives. For example, academic failure, ministerial failure, financial failure, career failure, marital failure, etc.

## PRAISE WORSHIP

## PRAYER WARFARE

1. I reject and denounce every spirit of failure, in Jesus' name
2. I bind every spirit of financial failure, in the name of Jesus.
3 I break every curse of automatic failure working in my family. back to ten generations on both sides of my family line, in the name of Jesus
4. I break every curse of failure, in the name of Jesus
5. Let all failures in the dream be converted to success, in Jesus' name.
6. I nullify all curses of failure in my, life in Jesus' name.
7. I pull down every stronghold of failure in my life, in Jesus' name.
8.. I pull down every stronghold of failure in my marriage, in the name of Jesus,

9. I pull down every stronghold of failure in my business, in the name of Jesus.

20. Every Pipeline of failure connected to my life, I command you to receive the fire of God and be consumed, in Jesus name.

21. Every spiritual barrier to success in my life, I command you to break into pieces, in the name of Jesus.

12. Every inherited and self-made failure in my life, I command you to receive repairs, in the name of Jesus.

13. Every seed of failure in my life, I command you to be consumed by the fire of God, in the name of Jesus.

14. Every area of my life that I have lost to failure, I command you to be restored, in Jesus' name.

15. You spirit of failure, loose your grip over my life, in Jesus name.

16 I refuse to register in the school of failure, in the mighty name of our Lord Jesus Christ

17. O Lord, let me not enter the trap of failure.

18. I remove my name from the book of failure and demonic side track, in the name of Jesus.

# 66

# SUICIDE SPIRITS

**INTRODUCTION**

These are spirits that initiate, sponsor and encourage people to end their own lives. These spirits mount terrible pressure on suicide victims. Many have fallen victims of these terrible spirits who order people to end their own lives quietly or violently.

## PRAISE WORSHIP

## PRAYER WARFARE

1. I release myself from the grip of the spirit of self-destruction, in the name of Jesus.
2 Power of the oppressor, release my spirit man, in Jesus' name.
3. My life, glorify the name of the Lord, in the name of Jesus.
4.. I will not terminate my own destiny, in the name of Jesus.
5. Every power encouraging me to end my life, die, in Jesus' name.
6. I bind and cast out every spirit of discouragement, in Jesus' name.
7. O God, arise and fight my battle for me, in Jesus' name.
8. I release myself from every generational suicidal-tendency, in the name of Jesus.
9. My Father, remove me from the cage of low esteem, in the name of Jesus.

10. I shall not give up, my problem shall give up, in Jesus name
11. I bind every evil voice speaking destruction to my life, in the name of Jesus.
12. Every strongman behind suicide I bind and pull you down, in the name of Jesus,
13. My Father, deliver me from hearing strange voices, in Jesus name.
14, Power of sudden death, loose your hold upon my life, in the name of Jesus
I5. Spirit of the living God, arise and pursue my pursuers, in the name of Jesus
16, I move from strength to strength by the power of God, in the name of Jesus.
17. My enemies shall not laugh last over my life, in Jesus' name.
18. I reject every internal pressure to end my life, in Jesus' name.
19 Let every internal warfare be quenched, in Jesus' name.
20. My life is not for sale, in the name of Jesus.
21. Every witchcraft agenda for my life, die, in Jesus' name.

# 67

# STRESS SPIRITS

## INTRODUCTION

These are demons responsible for physical and spiritual stress in people. They introduce situations and circumstances that look impossible and unachievable to the physical eyes. They cause restlessness, which makes people to age quickly.

## PRAISE WORSHIP

## PRAYER WARFARE

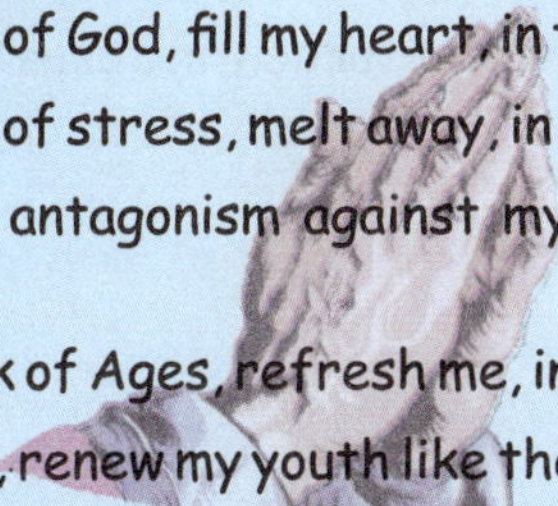

1. Power of God, fill my heart, in the name of Jesus.
2. Power of stress, melt away, in the name of Jesus.
3. Every antagonism against my health, be dismantled, in Jesus' name.
4. O Rock of Ages, refresh me, in the name of Jesus.
5. O God, renew my youth like the eagle's, in the name of Jesus.
6. I refuse to be stressed up, in the name of Jesus.
7. I receive deliverance from every power militating against my rest, in the name of Jesus.
8. O God, arise and let my deliverance come, in Jesus name.
9. Marks of stress go, marks of refreshment come, in Jesus name.
10. Power of God, pour your soothing oil over my life, in Jesus' name.
11. Holy Spirit, overshadow my spirit man, in Jesus name.

12. I bind and cast out every spirit of fear and worry from my life in the name of Jesus.
13. Holy spirit and fire fill my body, soul and spirit, in Jesus' name
14. Blood of Jesus, flow into my blood stream, in Jesus name..
15. I bind every power of fatigue and unexplainable tiredness, in the name of Jesus.
16. O Lord, let your living waters prolong my life, in Jesus name
17. I refuse to be cut off by the power of stress, in Jesus' name
18. Every arrow of stress backfire. in the name of Jesus
19. I shall not be a prey in the mouth of witchcraft lions, in the name of Jesus
20. My Father, move every stress out of my spirit, in Jesus name
21. I receive deliverance from the hands of the oppressors, in the name of Jesus
22. My life, reject every heavy yoke and burden, in Jesus name.

# 68

# REBELLION SPIRIT

## INTRODUCTION

The spirit of rebellion is very rampant these days. Unfortunately, the Bible equates rebellion with witchcraft. Rebellion against God and godly authority, has led many people into disaster

## PRAISE WORSHIP

## PRAYER WARFARE

1. Every spirit of rebellion I bind and cast you out, in Jesus name.
2. Every power that rebels against God, release my life, in the name of Jesus
3. I release my life from every yoke of rebellion, in Jesus name.
4 I repent from every rebellion against God, in Jesus' name.
5. I dismantle every apparatus of rebellion, in Jesus' name.
6. Holy Ghost fire, purge my life from every rebellion, in Jesus' name.
7. Spirit of obedience to God, come upon me, in Jesus' name.
8. I shall not be initiated into any form of witchcraft, in Jesus' name
9. Power of God, open my understanding, in the name of Jesus.

10. I shall not be diverted from my divine purpose,
11. My Father, pull me back from any path of rebellion, in Jesus' name
12. Every witchcraft power, loose your hold upon my life, in the name of Jesus.
13. Everything standing against the purpose of God for my life. be dismantled, in the name of Jesus.
14. My Glory and the Lifter of my head, release me from ever deception, in the name of Jesus.
15. I reject every evil handwriting moving my life towards disobedience to God, in the name of Jesus.
16. Holy Spirit, move upon my life in a new way, in Jesus name.
17. I shall be an overcomer over any evil temptation, in Jesus name
18. Wonderful God, incubate my life with your love, in Jesus name
19, O Lord, let me be in the right place at the right time, in the name of Jesus.
20. My God and my Father incubate my life by your power, in the name of Jesus.
21. I shall not be a child of perdition, in the name of Jesus.

# 69

# DESTRUCTIVE ADDICTION SPIRITS

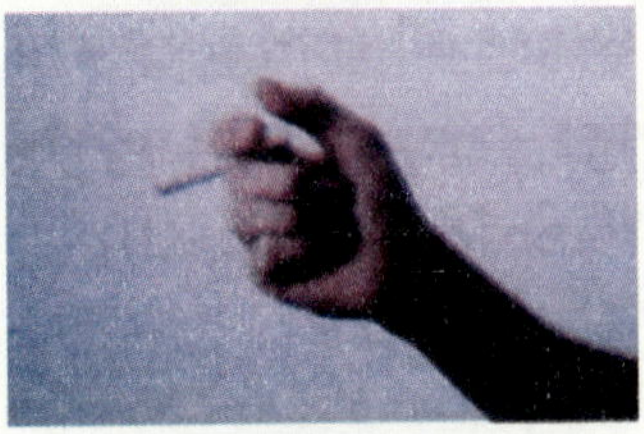

## INTRODUCTION

These are spirits responsible for all forms of destructive addictions. Whether it is sexual, alcoholic, work or drug addiction, it is still sponsored by these spirits. The spirit of addiction, hides away from one's view, the destructive consequences of one's action. All unrepentant drug addicts are time bombs waiting to explode.

## PRAISE WORSHIP

## PRAYER WARFARE

1. Father, I confess that in the past, I had been unforgiving, I harboured bitterness and resentment in my heart against certain people who had hurt or disappointed me.
2. I now recognise this as a sin and confess it as sin, for You have said in Your Word that if we confess our sins, You are faithful and just to forgive us our sins and to cleanse us of all unrighteousness (1 John 1:9).
3. I now forgive the following people, that I can remember, who had hurt or disappointed me. (Mention the names of those who come to your mind.) I now freely forgive all these people and ask You to bless them if they are still living.
4. I also forgive myself, for all my faults and failures, for You have freely forgiven me.

5. Thank You Father, for freedom from the load of unforgiveness, bitterness and resentment, in Jesus' name.

6. Father, I confess to You, that in the past, through ignorance, curiosity or wilfulness, I performed certain sinful acts. I now recognise these as sin and confess them as sin, and ask for forgiveness, in Jesus' name.

7. Specifically, I do confess as sin and renounce all contacts which I have had with the following occult things (mention everything in the occult, which you have dabbled into or involved with)

8 I also renounce and confess as sin, any oath which I made to any false god, and any idolatry in which I have been involved.

9. Satan, I rebuke you in the name of Jesus, and I close any door, which I or my ancestors opened to you and your demons, in the name of Jesus.

10, I renounce satan and all his demons; I declare them my enemies and I command them to get out of my life completely, in the name of Jesus.

11. In the name of Jesus Christ, I now claim deliverance from all evil spirits in me (Joel 2:28). Once and for all, I close the door in my life, to all occult practices and command all related spirits to leave me, in Jesus' name.

12. In the name of Jesus, I break any curse of rejection from the womb or illegitimacy in my family, even back to ten generations, on both sides of the family line (Deut. 26:2).

13. In the name of Jesus, I now renounce, break and loose myself from all demonic subjection, and any ungodly soul-tie to my mother, father, grandparents or any other person, living or dead, who have ever dominated or controlled me in any way contrary to

the will of God and God's word,

14. O Lord, I repent and ask You to forgive me, if I have ever dominated or controlled anybody in the wrong way

15. In the name of Jesus Christ, I now renounce, break and loose myself and all my descendants from all psychic heredity, demonic holds, psychic powers, bondage, bonds of physical or mental illness, or curses upon my family line as a result of sins, transgressions, iniquities, occult or psychic practices by me, my parents, or any of my ancestors, (my spouse, all ex-spouses, or their parents, or any of their ancestors)

16. In the name of Jesus Christ, I now renounce, break and loose myself and all my descendants from all evil curses, charms, hexes, spells, jinxes, psychic powers, bewitchments, witchcraft or sorcery, which may have been put upon us, by any person or persons, or from any occult or psychic source, I renounce all connected and related spirits and command them to leave me now.

17. I thank You Lord Jesus for setting me free.

18. In the name of Jesus Christ, I command satan and all his demons to loose their hold upon my mind completely.

19, I ask You Father to send Your angels to break, all fetters, bands, chains, and bonds of whatever sort the enemy has managed to place on my mind by word or deed.

20. I ask You, Father, to release to me and my family, these spirits of: wisdom, counsel, might, knowledge, fear of the Lord, power, love, sound mind, grace and peace.

21. Father, I break and renounce, all evil soul-ties with the free-masonry, religious systems, adulterers, drunkards, drug addicts,

close friends, cults, etc.

22. Father, I ask You, in the name of Jesus Christ, to send Your angels to gather up the fragments of my soul, and restore them to their rightful place in me. And break all earthen storage vessels, including all bonds or bands which have been put upon my soul by any means,

23. I claim the restoration of my soul

24, Let all the pieces of my fragmented mind, will and emotions be brought back into proper and original positions, in Jesus name.

25. In the name of Jesus Christ, I break all curses issued upon me by witchcraft, and command that, they and the spirits from them should return to the senders (Psalm 109:17,18),

26. According to Leviticus 26, I now confess the sins of my ancestors: idolatry, witchcraft, occultism, lust, adultery, divorce, perversion, pride, unbelief, rebellion and stubbornness.

27 I claim forgiveness, because of the provision in 1John 1:9;, O Lord, I declare the curses broken and lift them from me and my descendants.

28. I command all connected and related spirits to leave me and my family and go wherever Jesus wants them to go.

29. I confess that my body is the temple of the Holy Spirit redeemed, cleansed, and sanctified by the blood of Jesus Christ Therefore, Satan has no more place in me, no more power over me.

30 Satan, in the name of Jesus Christ the son of God, I put you and all your legions on notice, that I am attacking you from my position in Christ at the right hand of the Father in the third heaven. This, puts me high above you, your principalities, powers,

thrones, dominions, world rulers, rulers of darkness, kings, princes and every angelic rank under your command.

31. Confess Romans 8:15: "For I did not receive a spirit that makes one a slave again to fear (bondage); but I received the Spirit of sonship (adoption). And by Him I cry, Abba, Father."

32. Call the spirits you do not desire in your life by name. Then issue a command firmly and repeatedly that it should come out, in the name of the Lord Jesus.

33. Pray as follows: You spirit of addiction to, or craving for:

| | | | |
|---|---|---|---|
| - acid | - caffeine | - LSD | - peyote |
| - alcohol | - diepills | - - marijuana | - speed |
| - amphetamines | | - downers | - methadone |
| - STP | | - any drug | - hashish |
| - methedrine TM | | - sugar | - aspirin |
| -heroine | | - mood elevators | - tranquilizers |
| - barbiturates | | - junk food | - nicotine |

in the belly, in the blood, in the lungs, in the mind, in the sinuses, in the throat be paralysed, come out by fire, in the name of Jesus.

34. Pray as follows: You spirit of ....., come out of my brain and mind, in the name of Jesus.

| | | | |
|---|---|---|---|
| - binge | - greed | - nervousness | |
| - bulimia | - moodiness | - resentment | |
| - compulsiveness | | - self-reward | - restlessness |
| - frustration | - sweet tooth | | - self-pity |

39. I loose myself from you in the name of Jesus, and I command you to leave me right now, in the mighty name of our Lord Jesus Christ.

# 70

# SPIRIT OF POLYGAMY

## INTRODUCTION

This is a spirit responsible for multiple wives or husbands concubine, etc. This spirit causes disaffection and frustration monogamy, and has destroyed many promising destinies. It is the root of most divorce cases, re-marrying, early widowhood, etc

## PRAISE WORSHIP

## PRAYER WARFARE

1. Bring quality repentance unto the Lord for all sexual sins.
2. Every foundation of polygamy in my family line, break, in the name of Jesus
3. I refuse to follow the evil marital pattern of my fathers house. in the name of Jesus.
4. Every ancestral marital power caging my marriage, release me, in the name of Jesus.
5. Thou power of God, dismantle every polygamous witchcraft, in the name of Jesus.
6. Every evil immoral flow of my father's house, dry up, in the name of Jesus
7. Every spirit, sponsoring polygamy in my life, I bind you and cast you out, in the name of Jesus.

8. Every familiar spirit, targeting me for polygamy. I destroy your power, in the name of Jesus
9. Every magnet of polygamy. be destroyed by the power in the blood of Jesus.
10. Every curse and covenant of polygamy, break, in Jesus name.
11. Evil power of envious wives over my life, die, in Jesus name.
12. Evil plan of marital failure, be cancelled with the blood of Jesus.
13. Thou power of family idol, die, in the name of Jesus.
14. You stronghold of polygamy in my life, die, in Jesus name
15. Every problem connected to polygamy in my life, be solved by the blood of Jesus.
16. Let my destiny be released from the grip of polygamous power, in the name of Jesus.
17. Polygamous witchcraft embargo, die, in the name of Jesus.
18. Every evil plantation, acquired through polygamy, be uprooted, in the name of Jesus.
19. I bind and cast out every demon of lust in my life, in Jesus' name.
20. Every robbery of virtue, be cancelled, in the name of Jesus.
21. Marriage destroyers will not prosper in my life, in Jesus' name.
22. Every placental bondage, break, in the name of Jesus.
23. My foundation shall not disgrace my marriage, in Jesus' name.
24. Oppressive arrows of my father's wives, die, in Jesus' name.
25. Every war, waged on my mother that is now affecting me, die, in the name of Jesus.
26. My star, reject polygamous cages, in the name of Jesus

## PUBLICATIONS By DR. D. K. OLUKOYA, PUBLISHED AND MARKETED BY THE BATTLE CRY CHRISTIAN MINISTRIES

1. A-Z of Complete Deliverance
2. Be Prepared
3. Bewitchment must die
4. Biblical Principles of Dream Interpretation
5. Born Great, But Tied Down
6. Breaking Bad Habits
7. Breakthrough Prayers For Business Professionals
8. Brokenness
9. Bringing Down The Power of God
10. Can God Trust You?
11. Command The Morning
12. Consecration Commitment & Loyalty
13. Contending For The Kingdom
14. Connecting to The God of Breakthroughs
15. Criminals In The House Of God
16. Dealing With Hidden Curses
17. Dealing With Local Satanic Technology
18. Dealing With Satanic Exchange
19. Dealing With The Evil Powers Of Your Father's House
20. Dealing With Tropical Demons
21. Dealing With Unprofitable Roots
22. Dealing With Witchcraft Barbers
23. Deliverance By Fire
24. Deliverance From Spirit Husband And Spirit Wife
25. Deliverance From The Limiting Powers
26. Deliverance of The Brain
27. Deliverance Of The Conscience
28. Deliverance Of The Head
29. Deliverance: God's Medicine Bottle
30. Destiny Clinic
31. Destroying Satanic Masks
32. Disgracing Soul Hunters
33. Divine Military Training
34. Divine Yellow Card
35. Dominion Prosperity
36. Drawers Of Power From The Heavenlies

## PUBLICATIONS By DR. D. K. OLUKOYA, PUBLISHED AND MARKETED BY THE BATTLE CRY CHRISTIAN MINISTRIES

37. Evil Appetite
38. Evil Umbrella
39. Facing Both Ways
40. Failure In The School Of Prayer
41. Fire For Life's Journey
42. For We Wrestle..
43. Freedom Indeed
44. Holiness Unto The Lord
45. Holy Cry
46. Holy Fever
47. Hour Of Decision
48. How To Obtain Personal Deliverance
49. How To Pray When Surrounded By The Enemies
50. Idols Of The Heart
51. Is This What They Died For?
52. Let God Answer By Fire
53. Limiting God
54. Madness Of The Heart
55. Making Your Way Through The Traffic Jam of Life
56. Meat For Champions
57. Medicine For Winners
58. My Burden For The Church
59. Open Heavens Through Holy Disturbance
60. Overpowering Witchcraft
61. Paralysing The Riders And The Horse
62. Personal Spiritual Check-Up
63. Power Against Coffin Spirits
64. Power Against Destiny Quenchers
65. Power Against Dream Criminals
66. Power Against Local Wickedness
67. Power Against Marine Spirits
68. Power Against Spiritual Terrorists
69. Power Must Change Hands
70. Pray Your Way To Breakthroughs
71. Prayer Is The Battle
72. Prayer Rain
73. Prayer Strategies For Spinsters And Bachelors
74. Prayer To Kill Enchantment

## PUBLICATIONS By DR. D. K. OLUKOYA, PUBLISHED AND MARKETED BY THE BATTLE CRY CHRISTIAN MINISTRIES

75. Prayer To Make You Fulfil Your Divine Destiny
76. Prayer Warfare Against 70 Mad Spirits
77. Prayers For Open Heavens
78. Prayers To Arrest Satanic Frustration
79. Prayers To Destroy Diseases And Infirmities
80. Prayers To Move From Minium To Maximum
81. Prayers Against The Spirit Of The Valley
82. Praying To Destroy Satanic Roadblocks
83. Praying To Dismantle Witchcraft
84. Principles Of Prayer
85. Release From Destructive Covenants
86. Revoking Evil Decrees
87. Safeguarding Your Home
88. Satanic Diversion Of The Black Race
89. Silencing The Birds Of Darkness
90. Slaves Who Love Their Chains
91. Smite The Enemy And He will Flee
92. Speaking Destruction Unto The Dark Rivers
93. Spiritual Education
94. Spiritual Growth And Maturity
95. Spiritual Warfare And The Home
96. Strategic Praying
97. Strategy Of Warfare Praying
98. Stop Them Before They Stop You
99. Students in The School Of Fear
100. Symptoms Or Witchcraft Attack
101. The Baptism of Fire
102. The Battle Against The Spirit Of impossibility
103. The Dinning Table Of Darkness
104. The Enemy Has Done This
105. The Evil Cry Of Your Family Idol
106. The Fire Of Revival
107. The Great Deliverance
108. The Internal Stumbling Block
109. The Lord Is A Man Of War
110. The Mystery Of Mobile Curses
111. The Mystery Of The Mobile Temple
112. The Prayer Eagle

## PUBLICATIONS By DR. D. K. OLUKOYA, PUBLISHED AND MARKETED BY THE BATTLE CRY CHRISTIAN MINISTRIES

113. The Power of Aggressive Prayer Warriors
114. The Pursuit Of Success
115. The Seasons Of Life
116. The Secrets Of Greatness
117. The Serpentine Enemies
118. The Skeleton In Your Grandfather's Cupboard
119. The Slow Learners
120. The Snake In The Power House
121. The Spirit Of The Crab
122. The Star Hunters
123. The Star In Your Sky
124. The Terrible Agenda
125. The Tongue Trap
126. The Unconquerable Power
127. The Unlimited God
128. The Vagabond Spirit
129. The Way Of Divine Encounter
130. The Wealth Transfer Agenda
131. Tied Down In The Spirits
132. Too Hot To Handle
133. Turnaround Breakthrough
134. Unprofitable Foundations
135. Vacancy For Mad Prophets
136. Victory Over Satanic Dreams
137. Victory Over Your Greatest Enemies
138. Violent Prayers Against Stubborn Situations
139. War At The Edge Of Breakthroughs
140. Wasting The Wasters
141. Wealth Must Change Hands
142. What You Must Know About The House Fellowship
143. When God Is Silent
144. When the Battle is from Home
145. When The Deliverer Needs Deliverance
146. When Things Get Hard
147. When You Are Knocked Down
148. Where Is Your Faith
149. While Men Slept

## PUBLICATIONS By DR. D. K. OLUKOYA, PUBLISHED AND MARKETED BY THE BATTLE CRY CHRISTIAN MINISTRIES

150. Woman! Thou Art Loosed.
151. Your Battle And Your Strategy
152. Your Foundation And Destiny
153. Your Mouth And Your Deliverance
154. The Hour of Freedom
155. The Miracle of Divine Relocation
156. The Secret of Progress of Enlargement
157. Breaking the Power of the Past
158. Total Freedom and Deliverance
159. What to do When Trouble Comes
160. Deep Secret Deep Deliverance
161. When the Wicked is on Rampage
162. Discovering God's Purpose
163. When One Door Closes another Door Open
164. Power to Put the Enemy to Shame
165. Victory over Death
166. Prayers to Discover Your Treasure
167. Lost in the Church
168. Ways to Provoke Divine Vengeance
169. The Mystery of Dark Market
170. The Darkness of the Night
171. The Re-Possessing Power
172. The Mystery of Character
173. The Deep Truth about Marriage
174. Pulling Down Foundational Jericho
175. Victory over the Storms of Life
176. The Blood on the Door Post
177. Divine Compensation
178. Your Uzziah Must Die
179. Crucifixion of Poverty
180. Your Turn around Breakthrough
181. Divine Favour and Mercy
182. Watching the Serpents of the Magician
183. Wrestling with Shadows
184. Power Against Enemy Oppose To My Shining

## PUBLICATIONS By DR. D. K. OLUKOYA, PUBLISHED AND MARKETED BY THE BATTLE CRY CHRISTIAN MINISTRIES

185. Divine Repositioning
186. O God Terminate the Joy of my Enemy
187. Steps to Greatness
188. Deliverance from Multiple Bondage
189. The Tragedy of Stealing
190. Power to Achieve Success
191. The Power of Love
192. My Father Connect me to your Creative Power
193. God of 24 Hours Miracle Arise
194. The Mystery of Water Cure
195. Charge your Battery
196. Financial Deliverance
197. Deliverance from Triangular Power
198. The Mystery of Divine Connection
199. Power Against Anti breakthrough Power
200. My Life is not for Sale
201. Disgracing Water Spirit
202. The Militant Christian
203. The Lost Secret of the Church
204. Handling the Sword of Deliverance
205. Power against Business Bewitchment
206. Power through Fire Baptism
207. The Power of Excellence
208. I Plug Myself into The Socket Of Divine Favour
209. 214 Facts About Fear And Worry
210. The Gate Of Greatness
211. Hidden Areas Where Deliverance Is Needed
212. Breakthroughs Or Breakout
213. Dream Pointer
214. Your Past, Your Present And Your Future
215. The Price Of Power
216. The Word Heals.

### YORUBA PUBLICATIONS

1. ADURA AGBAYORI
2. ADURA TI NSI OKE NIDI
3. OJO ADURA

## PUBLICATIONS By DR. D. K. OLUKOYA, PUBLISHED AND MARKETED BY THE BATTLE CRY CHRISTIAN MINISTRIES

**FRENCH PUBLICATIONS**

1. PLUIE DE PRIERE
2. ESPIRIT DE VAGABONDAGE
3. EN FINIR AVEC LES FORCES MALEFIOUES DE LA MAISON DE TON PERE
4. QUE I'ENVOUTEMENT PERISSE
5. FRAPPEZI'ADVERSAIRE ET IL FUIRA
6. COMMENT RECEVIOR LA DELVRANCE DU MARI ET FEMME DE NUIT
7. CPMMENT SE DELUVRER SO-MEME
8. POVOIR CONTRE LES TERRORITES SPIRITUEL
9. PRIERE DE PERCEES POUR LES HOMMES D'AFFAIRES
10. PRIER JUSQU'A REMPORTER LA VICTOIRE
11. PRIERES VIOLENTES POUR HUMILIER LES PROBLEMES OPINIATRES
12. PRIERE POUR DETRUIRE LES MALADIES ET INFIRMITES
13. LE COMBAT SPIRITUEL ET LE FOYER
14. BILAN SPIRITUEL PERSONNEL
15. VICTOIRES SUR LES REVES SATANIQUES
16. PRIERES DE COMAT CONTRE 70 ESPIRITS DECHANINES
17. LA DEVIATION SATANIQUE DE LA RACE NOIRE
18. TON COMBAT ET TA STRATEGIE
19. VOTRE FONDEMENT ET VOTRE DESTIN
20. REVOQUER LES DECRETS MALEFIQUES
21. CANTIQUE DES CONTIQUES
22. LE MAUVAIS CRI DES IDOLES
23. QUAND LES CHOSES DEVIENNENT DIFFICILES
24. LES STRATEGIES DE PRIERES POUR LES CELIBATAIRES
25. SE LIBERER DES ALLIANCES MALEFIQUES
26. DEMANTELER LA SORCELLERIE

## PUBLICATIONS By DR. D. K. OLUKOYA, PUBLISHED AND MARKETED BY THE BATTLE CRY CHRISTIAN MINISTRIES

27. LA DELIVERANCE: LE FLACON DE MEDICAMENT DIEU
28. LA DELIVERANCE DE LA TETE
29. COMMANDER LE MATIN
30. NE GRAND MAIS LIE
31. POUVOIR CONTRE LES DEMOND TROPICAUX
32. LE PROGRAMME DE TRANFERT DE RICHESSE
33. LES ETUDIANTSAIECOLE DE LA PEUR
34. L'ETOILE DANS VOTRE CIEL
35. LES SAISONS DE LA VIE
36. FEMME TU ES LIBEREE

**ANNUAL 70 DAYS PRAYER AND FASTING PUBLICATIONS**

1. Prayers That Bring Miracles
2. Let God Answer By Fire
3. Prayers To Mount With Wings As Eagles
4. Prayers That Bring Explosive Increase
5. Prayers For Open Heavens
6. Prayers To Make You Fulfil Your Divine Destiny
7. Prayers That Make God To Answer And Fight By Fire.
8. Prayers That Bring Unchallengeable Victory And Breakthrough Rainfall Bombardments

## BOOKS BY PASTOR (MRS) SHADE OLUKOYA

1. Power To Fulfil Your Destiny
2. Principles Of A Successful Marriage
3. The Call of God
4. The Daughters of Phillip
5. When Your Destiny is Under Attack
6. Violence Against Negative Voices
7. Woman of Wonder
8. I Decree An Uncommon Change